PICTORIAL POULTRY-KEEPING

PICTORIAL
POULTRY-KEEPING

Revised by

Dr. J. Batty

THIRD EDITION

PUBLISHED BY SPUR PUBLICATIONS
SAIGA PUBLISHING CO. LTD.
1 Royal Parade
Hindhead, Surrey

Published by:
SAIGA PUBISHING CO. LTD.,
1 Royal Parade, Hindhead,
Surrey GU26 6TD, England.

Printed and bound in Great Britain
at The Pitman Press, Bath

CONTENTS

INTRODUCTION

THOUGH times favour the bigger farmer, the success of the first edition of Pictorial Poultry-Keeping shows that there are still many thousands of small poultry-keepers who require practical information on all aspects of production. Breeding, incubation and so on remain of interest to a large number of such producers: handling and culling of individual birds is still an important factor for the small flock owner. That is why these aspects of poultry-keeping are again covered in this second edition, while the illustrations and text both take account of the fact that most small producers have to do the best they can with workaday housing and equipment rather than "hen palaces".

POULTRY

WHAT *is* it about poultry? While economists reiterate that small poultry farmers must expect a bleak future, and at a time when many *larger* table poultry producers have decided to cut their losses, there are still many, many thousands of laying units consisting of between a few dozen and a few hundred birds. And as fast as their owners decide either to expand, or to stop keeping poultry, there always seems to be an equal number of newcomers ready and waiting to fill their ranks.

The truth is that there is no finer means of breaking into the livestock field than by keeping poultry. They are reasonably easy to handle and manage, do not necessarily require great capital outlay—yet always they will repay that extra care and skill which the smaller poultry keeper is best placed to give. So if you want to keep poultry, go right ahead. Don't take too much notice of the pessimists. Even so, remember that a modest start pays best, whether or not you hope to expand later.

WHAT POULTRY-KEEPING OFFERS

On a Back-garden Scale . . .

THOUGH most people start keeping poultry for the sake of having fresh eggs, a great many find that their stock provides such interest that their garden would seem incomplete without them. There is something to be proud of in a pen of vigorous young pullets which, thanks to your good feeding and management, are laying that little bit better than your next-door neighbour's. And then there's the excitement of finding the first egg of the season and watching the daily score rise, till peak production is reached. Well-managed birds will give up to 200 eggs or more each year.

Egg-production is the aim of most back-garden poultry-keepers but the layers must be replaced every year or two. The birds to be disposed of will make a really delicious meal, either boiled or roasted in a very slow oven.

If you do not already keep poultry, ask yourself, "How long is it since I had a really fresh egg?" No, not a "new laid" egg from the grocer but one which was laid only twenty-four hours before you eat it. It may well be that you have forgotten just what a contrast there is between the two but this difference alone is sufficient to make poultry-keeping worth while.

. . . And for the Commercial Producer

Commercial poultry-keeping, while demanding adequate capital and skill, offers a life full of interest, with opportunity for initiative and business ability. In normal times, poultry-keeping will provide a reasonable living for the efficient producer who can combine a good level of production with economical running costs. A small, well-planned farm can often be run by a man and his wife, without employing labour.

There are many branches and systems of poultry-keeping. Ducks, geese and turkeys offer interesting alternatives to the keeping of fowls for eggs or table bird production. But it must be borne in mind that most successful poultry-keepers are specialists and there is certainly no room for "dabblers". So beginners should take expert advice before investing precious capital.

... *What it Entails*

Livestock are not machines: however well-organised, a poultry farm cannot be run entirely on factory lines. Stock-sense is a quality which comes with experience to those with a genuine interest in, and feeling for, livestock. It is needed constantly in the handling of poultry, in culling the wasters, in spotting feeding deficiencies and in noticing, *before* harm has been done, when all is not quite as it should be with the flock.

As this implies, a reasonable degree of experience is needed before attempting to keep poultry on a commercial scale. Many poultry-farmers first learned the elements of management with a back-garden flock.

Like all livestock, poultry need feeding and tending every single day of the year. True, with certain systems it is possible to leave the birds for a day without any harm being done but such a practice should be reserved for emergencies. The man who succeeds with poultry is the one who puts his stock first—wet or dry, sun or snow—the whole year round.

SYSTEMS OF POULTRY-KEEPING
Semi-intensive Housing

THE semi-intensive system allows the birds to live naturally with grass and adequate natural lighting and, of course, plenty of fresh air. Its main disadvantages are that runs may become 'sour' and in inclement weather the birds have to be kept indoors or egg production will be adversely affected. For pullet rearing or for keeping a small flock of a breed the system is ideal. It is excellent for the person who wishes to have free-range eggs.

Under the semi-intensive system each bird is allowed up to 4 sq. ft. of floor space in the house and has, in addition, access to a grass run. About 18 sq. yds. of run space per bird (spread over two runs) is generally adequate and rather less than this may be allowed for light breeds on light, well-drained soil. Success with this system will depend in large measure on having two runs for each house, or section of a large house, as in the photograph above, so that while one is occupied the other can be rested.

In all but the most severe weather the birds are free to come and go between the house and the run as they wish. This undoubtedly makes for healthy and reasonably hardy stock and the interest provided by the grass and change of surroundings assists materially in cutting down such vices as feather-pecking.

Housing costs are less than when a fully-intensive system is adopted.

Against these considerations must be reckoned a rather lower output than when the birds are completely shielded from the weather, while control of the grass runs may call for labour during the spring and summer. For winter egg-production, semi-intensive housing is most suited to the southern counties or at any rate to farms where there is some degree of natural protection from the coldest winds.

The Strawyard or Henyard

After a spell of popularity, strawyards have tended to go out of favour during the past few years. But the system has much to commend it and is well worth considering. It might be described as a semi-intensive unit in which a strawed and adequately protected yard takes the place of a grass run, with just sufficient housing on one side to keep the birds out of the weather and provide roosting, feeding and laying facilities. An open-fronted shed is frequently used for the purpose (the front can be partly covered in winter) but in any case about 2 sq. ft. per bird should be allowed under cover, while the yard space needed is 5 or 6 sq. ft. per bird.

Strawyards must be built on really well-drained land and it is essential for economic running that a cheap and plentiful supply of straw be available. For 50 birds, a ton or more of straw will be needed in the course of a year. The yards are cleaned out annually, fresh straw being added as each layer becomes soiled or sodden. If natural protection is not available, cheap surrounding walls can be built by ramming straw between two layers of wire-netting, as in the photograph.

Another very helpful factor may be the availability of a disused shed or similar building, which can be converted at little cost. Make-shift strawyards are generally more satisfactory than make-shift deep litter houses as there are not the ventilation problems.

Birds penned in yards generally keep in excellent health, and production during the winter is good. Capital outlay and labour are moderate. In areas where straw is very expensive, pebble yards have been tried with very good results. Except during prolonged dry weather, when washing down may be needed, they keep reasonably clean. Clinker and sand yards have been tried but pebbles are probably best.

The Intensive House

Intensive housing of one sort or another is now considered essential by the majority of specialist egg producers. The original purpose of providing protection from the weather has been developed to the extent where the whole environment—temperature, light and ventilation—can be controlled at optimum levels. By this means a high rate of production can be maintained, and growing pullets brought to maturity, regardless of the season, and the health and well-being of the stock kept under closer control.

However, a fully-controlled environment is by no means essential for profitable production. The main requirements of an intensive house are a reasonable degree of insulation and adequate ventilation.

Nowadays, most intensive houses have either a deep litter floor and droppings pit or else have part or the whole of the floor covered with wire mesh or slats. There is no general agreement as to which system is best though it is true that slats and wire floors permit a much heavier rate of stocking. On the other hand, the more intensive the system the greater the risk of vices, such as feather picking, and of outbreaks of respiratory diseases, unless management is of a high standard.

Hybrids and light breeds kept on deep litter need about $3\frac{1}{2}$ sq. ft. per bird (for flocks of 100). On slatted or wire floors the space requirement is only about $1\frac{1}{2}$ sq. ft. If a third of the floor area is occupied by a droppings pit, with the rest littered, about 2 sq. ft. per bird is needed. For heavy breeds a little more space is recommended: the same applies when birds are penned in flocks of 50 or less.

Whether the floor is littered or wire-covered, cleaning-out is an annual operation. The labour requirement is much the same in either case. But a big advantage of slats and wire is that there are no problems with damp or dusty litter during the laying season. It seems likely that an increasing number of egg-producers will turn to these 'super-intensive' systems, or at least arrive at a compromise by covering a large part of the floor area with slats or wire.

(*Courtesy*: R.J. Patchett Ltd.)

Laying Cages

Though the capital involved in this highly intensive system is considerable, the method does offer a number of advantages. First and foremost, it gives you full control over each bird and it is impossible for the poor layers to go undetected. A large flock can be kept on a small area of land. Finally, if properly fed and managed, battery birds are nearly always better egg producers than those kept under more natural conditions.

The batteries themselves must be situated in a well-lit, properly-ventilated building. Allow a gangway 3 ft. wide all round the cages as well as several feet of space between the top tier and the roof.

Fold Units

Though fold units are primarily a means of housing poultry on the general farm, and are hard to beat where they are considered as just one item in the general rotation, the system is most accommodating in that it can be used for birds of all ages, from the rearing to the laying stage, and is also suitable for breeding pens. Success with folds will, however, depend on having sufficient land to move the folds to fresh ground every day (without returning to the same spot for a month or more) and the land should also be of medium to light quality if a full rate of stocking is to be achieved all the year round. Under normal conditions this means about 200 birds to the acre, divided into units of 20 to 25.

An outstanding advantage of folds is that they do give full protection against foxes. In certain districts, it has become impossible to keep a free-range flock because of these animals and folds are undoubtedly the answer.

The fact that the birds are kept in relatively small groups makes for effective control of disease and allows speedy and efficient observation. The birds' droppings have an excellent effect on the sward and the distribution is, of course, more even than when a large flock is ranging from a number of centrally-placed houses, when damage to the sward may also occur.

On the debit side is the fairly considerable cost of well-made fold units and their somewhat high rate of depreciation in value. Cheap, shoddily-made folds should be avoided at all costs. They also take rather a lot of labour and when many units are involved it is necessary to have some easy means of carrying food and water supplies.

Under favourable conditions, winter egg-production can be reasonably good, though never comparing with fully-intensive housing. It is mainly for this reason that the system has lost popularity in recent years.

Many types of fold are now marketed but units about 20 ft. long by 5 ft. wide, holding from 20 to 25 birds have proved excellent in practice. Make sure that whatever you buy can be moved easily, offers a reasonable degree of protection to the birds and is soundly made of robust materials.

Range Housing

To a certain extent, what was said on the previous page about fold units is also true of the free-range system. Both are of greatest use to the general farmer and for range houses, especially, there is little place on the smallholding. However, on a great many farms they are used in conjunction with fenced runs and this method is reasonably successful if adequate run space is provided to make up for the cramped roosting quarters.

It is open to question, however, whether the purchase of new range housing for use in this way is justified when winter egg-production is the main consideration. Experience has shown that yields from birds kept on more intensive lines, or in henyards, are substantially greater and any capital saving is generally soon discounted.

Land heavily-stocked with poultry for a number of years becomes sour and will inevitably lead to serious losses from disease. When it is realised that the rate of stocking on the free range system, averaged throughout the year, should be between 50 and 100 birds per acre, it can be understood that this is essentially a system for the larger farm. Again, the houses should be fairly well spread out (farther apart, for preference, than in the photograph above), and this again underlines the need for adequate space.

Range houses are of two types—those with solid floors and those with slatted floors. The latter have the advantage of cheapness and are also probably the healthier of the two, but the solid floor houses may be used, without adaptation, for all classes of stock and provide better protection from the weather. On balance, the slatted floor house is more popular in most areas.

Both types of house should be fitted with wheels or skids—the latter for preference on any but light land—as it is important to move the houses at frequent intervals to prevent fouling the land in the vicinity of the house and to make full use of whatever range is available.

Free range conditions are definitely more suited to fairly sheltered areas and it is also of importance that the district should not be one overrun with foxes. In most cases the best use for such housing on small farms is for accommodating growing or breeding stock and not for housing the laying flock whose winter production is of such fundamental importance.

Poultry in the Garden

Back-garden poultry-keeping achieved its greatest popularity during and immediately after the last war, but there are still plenty of householders who prefer to produce their own eggs. For a modest outlay a house of pleasing appearance can be built or purchased and feeding costs can be kept at quite a low level, if house scraps form the basis of the ration. These must be balanced with a high-protein meal.

Fresh eggs and the occasional table bird, as well as valuable manure for the garden, are obvious returns for the outlay and labour involved, but it must be remembered that the birds will need attention the whole year round and some arrangement must be made for feeding them at holiday times. If fresh pullets are bought in each year, it is often possible to dispose of the yearlings before one goes on holiday and to arrange for delivery of the pullets on one's return.

The half-dozen or so layers favoured by most domestic poultry-keepers should achieve a very high rate of production. The individual care, and attention to detail, which is possible with such a small number, often results in more eggs per bird than the specialist poultry-farmer can achieve. This very fact has led many domestic poultry-keepers to the dangerous assumption that by increasing their flock to, say, 100, their profit would rise in like manner.

Types of house are numerous but by far the most popular is a miniature edition of the semi-intensive system, a small covered run being attached to the sleeping quarters. The latter should be large enough to allow at least limited scratching space during very severe weather. It is also a distinct advantage to have the weather side of the run covered, as well as the roof and the farthest end from the house. Alternatively, the outfit may be placed against a hedge or wall.

A common practice is that of raising the house some distance from the ground so as to allow the stock room beneath. In this way, a pen of about six laying birds can be kept on an area of as little as 40 sq. ft. Alternatively, small intensive houses and battery units are available for those who prefer such systems.

Some domestic poultry-keepers rear their own replacement stock from the day-old stage. This greatly adds to the interest of the undertaking but do make sure that you have enough space to house both the growers and the laying pullets until the latter are disposed of.

A Well-designed Back-Garden Unit

HOUSING AND APPLIANCES
Semi-intensive System

THE semi-intensive system is not the most labour-saving method of keeping poultry, but by thoughtful design and planning it is possible to save a lot of unnecessary work.

Tractors are now in common use on even quite small farms and the special gateway above is designed to provide ample room for a tractor and trailer but without the need to open a wide gate each time the poultryman passes. The hinged centre section is intended for this purpose while the whole structure lifts from its framework to allow a tractor to pass through.

Pop-holes need not be draught holes. Porches like those below are easily made and are a boon when cold winds threaten to affect egg-production.

Pop-hole Covers are Easily Constructed

Moveable Shelter

In exposed runs it pays to provide some form of shelter against wind. This is equally important whether growers, layers or breeding birds are penned. This simple device made of sheet metal on a timber frame can be moved to suit the wind direction. Picture on the right shows a bricked area around the house entrance which prevents this much-used area from becoming a mud bath. Result—happier birds and cleaner eggs. It also makes life a good deal pleasanter for the poultryman during winter.

Dry Underfoot

Perch Design

This perch design (*right*) is often seen in small houses, the near side being hooked up to allow the droppings board to be cleaned. Note that the walls have been lime-washed to brighten the interior.

Strawyards

Both photographs show how use can be made of existing structures when designing a henyard. Above, an old open-fronted shed, formerly used for storage and implements, needed only a substantial perch unit to complete it.

In this case a south-facing wall has been used as the basis for a similar layout. In both instances, added protection for the winter would be needed in more exposed districts. Note the generous trough space and the sheet metal guard to keep the birds from the droppings pit beneath the perches.

Feed under Cover

Birds in strawyards are often fed under cover and the water supply should always be in a sheltered position. The usual system, when pellets or a dry mash are fed, is to provide hoppers which hold sufficient food for one day. Community nest boxes or laying rooms are also in general use and assist further in cutting down labour.

Covered Strawyard

This unusual set-up is what might be called a strawyard under cover. The grower decided that winter eggs might give better returns than market produce and, in common with others who have tried the same scheme, found that production was good. Ventilation must be generous and the birds removed in good time in the spring before hot weather arrives.

Intensive Houses

Intensive housing is expensive and it is important to make use of every inch of floor space. In the small house (*above*) all fittings are raised from the floor so that the birds have free access beneath. Houses should not be less than 12–14 ft. wide as the stock may become nervous in a narrow house at feeding times.

Larger Houses

Large intensive houses should be divided into sections: it has been found that better results are obtained when birds are run in groups of not more than 300 each. With dry feeding a 20 ft. trough (double sided) is sufficient for each 100 laying pullets. In the case of tubular feeders, provide four per 100 layers.

Droppings Pit

A good deal of routine labour can be saved by placing the perches over a droppings pit instead of a board. The droppings are allowed to accumulate and are cleaned out only once or twice a year. The birds are kept from scratching in the droppings by large-mesh wire-netting fixed beneath the perches and down to the floor.

Simple Remedy

If double-sided nest boxes are installed the layers will soon find the ridge a convenient perch and the surface will become soiled with their droppings as a result. Photo on the left shows one simple way of stopping the trouble.

Community Nest box

Community nest boxes of the tunnel type (*seen below*) are a great help in preventing egg-eating. They are also labour-saving. The opening should be in the centre of each compartment, or at both ends, with a roomy landing ledge outside. Some means of closing the nest at night is also desirable though this must be opened again after the birds have gone to roost. A compartment 5 ft. long by 2 ft. wide is sufficient for up to 50 layers.

Modern Housing

MODERN housing is designed specifically for keeping poultry in an intensive manner. Special attention is paid to the needs of the birds so that they have adequate lighting and ventilation. In the illustration given above it will be noted that the large house is fitted with cowls for ventilation and inside there would be large fans to regulate air flow and temperature.

There are no windows because the exact light pattern for maximum production can be best obtained by the use of artificial light.

Automatic feeding is a feature of modern building design and the illustration given below shows the large food hopper which is used for bulk storage. Because of the need to save costs, the emphasis in the poultry industry has been to devise labour-saving ideas; yet giving the exact food, water and physical condition requirements.

(*Courtesy*: Harlow Bros. Ltd., *photos courtesy*: Smith's Studios Ltd.)

Cleaning Droppings Trays

Though very small battery units do not justify the expense of mechanical aids for cleaning the droppings trays, some such system becomes well worth while when a large number of birds are kept in cages.

The method varies with the make of cage, a popular one being that seen on the right. In this the droppings fall on to a length of felt. This passes under each tier of cages and can be wound on to the rollers at either end of the row where a spring-loaded scraper removes the droppings, allowing them to fall into a box or barrow.

In other systems, a windlass-drawn scraper is drawn down the whole length of the row; in this case the droppings tray is made of metal. Yet another method is to collect the droppings on long lengths of tough paper.

Outdoor Batteries

Outdoor batteries have never become really popular. The extra cost of housing is likely to be justified by improved and consistent egg yields. However, if outdoor batteries are used the important thing is to provide as much natural protection as possible,

Modern Cages

Modern cages try to include all features necessary for maximum production. For example:
(a) constant supply of food;
(b) nipples for water which eliminate the need for drinking fountains.

(*Courtesy*:
R.J. Patchett Ltd.)

Californian Cages

The Californian cages exhibited possess many advantages. An important feature is the fact that droppings fall into a pit below the cages, and, therefore, they are quite labour saving. Periodically the pit is cleaned out and pressure washed.

(*Courtesy*:
R.J. Patchett Ltd.)

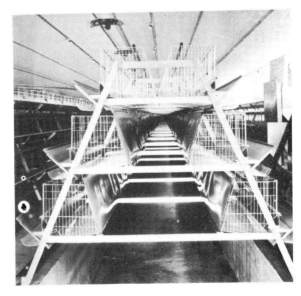

Range Houses

Slatted-Floor Unit

The typical slatted-floor unit above is being used on the semi-intensive principle, the birds being confined to a run. However, a greater run area is needed than with the normal type of semi-intensive house as a fully-stocked slatted-floor house provides roosting and laying quarters only. Some designs allow for feed and water troughs beneath the nest boxes, and this is quite satisfactory providing only dry meal or pellets are fed. Failing this, it is usual to provide the feed in weatherproof, conical hoppers.

Although the colony-type house is not much in favour nowadays, it is likely to prove better for winter egg production than the slatted-floor house. The rate of stocking is mainly dependent on ventilation and for the lean-to type of colony house (*below*) not less than 3 sq. ft. should be allowed per bird. On the other hand, a well-designed house with a centre ridge and baffled air inlets should accommodate up to twice as many layers.

Colony-Type House

Home-Made Housing

Many poultry farmers who rear on range have designed and made their own arks and rearing houses. The simple shelters seen above have asbestos roofs and slatted floors. They are light enough for easy movement at frequent intervals to fresh ground. In these and other arks it is common practice to remove the ridge caps during very hot weather so as to improve ventilation—always the limiting factor to stocking rates in poultry houses of all types.

Slatted-Floor House Interior

This close-up of the interior of a slatted-floor house shows how excellent is the ventilation. Because of this it can be stocked at the rate of 1 sq. ft. per bird, or even less. The drop-

pings trays underneath the slats are removable for cleaning. It is usual to have the under-side of the slats narrower than the top so as to prevent droppings lodging between, and clogging, the spaces.

The floor is generally made in sections so that it can be taken out and cleaned. The nest boxes are positioned on either side of the house and can be opened from outside.

Moving Fold Units

It is usual to move folds by hand but a tractor is sometimes employed to speed the task. This brings home the need for strength in design, for the job must be done daily, year in and year out. However, if the folds are to be moved by hand, the question of weight is also of importance and this is a point in favour of some of the aluminium folds on the market.

The sleeping compartment generally has a slatted floor, though strong wire floors are also used with success. There must be provision on one side of the run for the attendant to enter and it is usual to have the far end of the run covered over so that the food trough can be placed beneath in bad weather. Nest boxes, either separate or communal, are situated in the sleeping compartment.

Water Provision

Water is best provided in a bucket suspended from the top ridge of the fold. It is easily removed for cleaning and re-filling and cannot be upset. Most folds have a broody coop fitted in the pen to save the inconvenience of having to move birds long distances from the fold to the farm.

Back-garden Housing

These three pictures of domestic units, all home-made, give some idea of the designs which can be thought up to suit individual tastes and needs. In each case space has been provided for the birds to scratch about in during the day.

Avoid Eyesores

There is really no excuse for eyesores made of odd scraps of material and bits of tin. Such erections earn a bad name for domestic poultry-keeping and the birds housed in them are less likely to get good attention than when the owner can take a justifiable pride in his hobby.

Common Difficulty—

Many people who would like to keep poultry in their gardens as a hobby are deterred because they are out at work all day or are unable to give the birds regular attention. Others have very little space in which to put a house and run.

—Batteries the Answer

In both cases batteries can provide a perfectly satisfactory solution, for sufficient food and water can be given to last the birds throughout the day and the batteries can be housed in an outhouse or shed or disused garage, providing that ventilation receives due attention. The egg-eating vice—a common trouble when eggs are not collected regularly from the nest—will also be avoided.

Outdoor Batteries

These are more suited to garden conditions than those on the farm, for the degree of natural protection is likely to be greater. Points to note in the picture (right) are the covers over the front of the feeding troughs, the excellent protection afforded the birds and the rat guards on each leg of the unit.

If you think of trying to make such a unit yourself the approximate dimensions for each cage should be 18 in. deep, 15 in. wide and 14 in. high at the back, sloping to 18 in. in the front.

The neat unit in the lower photo has sliding glass panels across the front to allow variable ventilation.

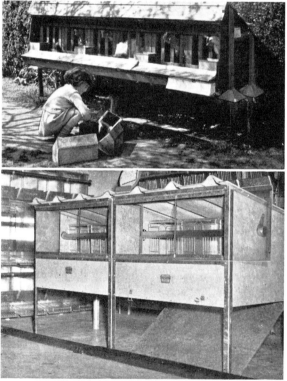

Well Protected

LITTER FOR HOUSE AND RUN

Very variable results have been achieved with the deep litter system—one of the reasons why wire floors have become so popular. But in most cases of failure, a little more attention to insulation and ventilation would make a good deal of difference. Likewise, extension of the droppings pit area.

Floor Litter

Some form of floor litter is needed in solid floor houses and in small covered runs. Its purpose is to absorb and cover the birds' droppings, to provide a certain amount of insulation underfoot and to give the birds a suitable medium in which to scratch for grain (*top right*).

For covered runs in garden units (bottom photo) baled straw is suitable but for deep litter the most popular material is wood shavings (centre) often mixed with varying proportions of chopped straw and/or peat moss.

Following are general notes on litter for various purposes:

Peat Moss: Expensive but very absorbent. If good quality (not dusty) peat moss can be had at a reasonable cost, then well worth buying.

Wood Shavings: Excellent though sometimes in short supply.

Chaff: Best used on top of peat moss.

Cut Straw: Very useful, especially for chick brooding. If used on its own for adult birds a generous depth is needed.

Sand, Sawdust: Good chick litter but must be quite dry.

Dried Bracken, Leaves: Worth using if they can be collected easily and in substantial quantities.

Baled Straw

Loosening the Litter

Deep Litter House

Management of deep litter houses (*below*) starts when new litter is put in prior to introducing the new season's pullets. Wood shavings are as good a material as any to start with (these can be mixed, if desired, with peat moss, chaff, chopped straw, etc.) and an initial depth of 4 in. is sufficient. This should be added to at intervals throughout the year until the depth has been doubled.

Bad Ventilation

If the litter becomes too damp, insufficient ventilation is often to blame. Trouble may also occur when the house is badly insulated as condensation is likely under such conditions. Lining the interior walls and roof with insulation board is not very expensive but it can make a great difference to results. Deep litter is difficult to start in cold weather, when bacterial action is slow.

The litter must be loosened whenever it tends to form a crust, and it is a good idea to move the feeding and drinking stands a little each week.

Earth Floors

Earth floors are probably best for deep litter houses but in this case the earth inside the building must be isolated from the exterior by sheets of iron sunk into the ground, etc. Wood floors give quite good results and many barn lofts have been converted for deep litter with every success.

Deep Litter House

THINGS TO MAKE YOURSELF

Straw Houses

STRAW is a cheap building material and a good insulator. Some skill is needed to build the neat semi-intensive type of house in the top photo but anyone can ram straw between two layers of netting (2 in. apart) to make the very effective building seen below. Use 2 in. × 2 in. timber framing and cover with roofing felt.

Egg Indicator

Special indicators can be bought to mark up the egg score of each battery layer, or each egg collected can be marked on a card. But perhaps the quickest and cheapest device is an ordinary clothes peg, this being moved one space to the right for every egg laid. If eggs tend to crack on the end guard, fasten springy curtain wire just behind.

Foot-scraper

Dirty eggs sell for less money and even if they are cleaned they often remain stained. Best way is to stop them getting dirty. This foot-scraper, made of heavy gauge netting, helps to prevent dirt being carried into the house.

Self-feeder

Oil-drum into self-feeder is the theme of the right-hand photo. A variety of designs is possible but this one is so made that the weight of the birds on the perching slats opens the feeding flap. At other times it remains closed to keep out damp and vermin.

A Handy Fold

In most gardens there are odd pieces of wood which can be put to some useful purpose. The fold above was made of such material, with the addition of a little roofing felt, and is excellent housing for growing stock, sick birds, table cockerels, etc., when normal housing is not available. End of the covered section has been removed to show the slatted floor.

Easy Cleaning

The photographs left and centre show how a house can be adapted to make it easier to clean the droppings board. Part of the rear wall of the house is hinged (to the same width as the board) and is held secure by a chain when raised. The droppings board, arrowed in both photos, is also hinged to assist cleaning. The hinged section of the wall must fit snugly otherwise there will be dangerous draughts.

Deep litter equipment can be made by any handyman. Note the legs of the feeding trough and water vessel below; these must rest on the floor of the house, not on top of the litter. A spinner is fitted above the trough and there is a perch on either side. The trough lifts out of the end framework for cleaning.

The box in which the water vessel rests (the latter is a cut down oil drum, incidentally) should be tarred or lined with roofing felt so that water flicked out or spilled by the birds does not fall through to make the litter damp.

Deep Litter Equipment

UTILITY POULTRY BREEDS

POPULAR HEAVY BREEDS

Light Sussex and Rhode Island Red

THE Light Sussex (above) is a utility breed, being quite a good layer and yet having sufficient flesh to make it suitable for the table. A cock should weigh around 9 lb. The colour is predominantly white with the neck hackle striped with black. This bird belongs to a family of Sussex which includes Browns, Buffs, Reds, Speckled Silver and White. This breed is very useful for providing broody hens.

Rhode Island Reds originated in the U.S.A. They are very respectable layers of light brown eggs and yet are also suitable for producing roast chicken. The colour varies from a fawny-red to a very deep chocolate-red — essential in show specimens. Rhode Island Reds are extremely attractive birds and they are quite easy to manage.

The Marans

The Marans breed deserves inclusion in this review of utility poultry because of the superb rich brown colour of its eggs. Where only a small flock of layers is kept, and their eggs sold by personal contacts, this can be a real selling point. It is also an attractive bird to look at with its barred plumage. There are three varieties of the breed in this country — Dark, Gold, and Silver.

As regards the number of eggs produced, this cannot be said to compare with the more highly-developed strains of Rhode Island Red or Light Sussex. In any case, it has been shown that when the Marans is bred for higher egg production the colour of the eggs almost invariably suffers. On the other hand, the breed is very useful for table purposes, giving a white carcase of medium size.

The White Wyandotte

The Wyandotte is also a dual purpose breed being both a layer and a table bird. At one time the breed was very popular, offering a wide variety of standardised colours. Although the Silver Laced was the first variety introduced from the U.S.A., the White Wyandotte was probably the most popular. In recent times there has been a revival of a number of the colours which had disappeared.

Buff Rock

The Buff Rock and the Barred Rock are both useful dual-purpose breeds but the Buff Rock (*above*) is the more popular and there are a number of excellent utility strains. Noted for its hardiness, it is capable of a high output of eggs (tinted) and gives a useful carcase which is spoiled only by its yellow skin. A breed, this, for those who wish to combine utility qualities with something a little different from the more popular and publicised breeds.

Barred Rock

This breed (*left*) has never achieved the popularity over here that it has won for itself in Canada and the U.S.A., and there is no doubt that type varies considerably on either side of the Atlantic. A fairly common fault is the production of under-sized eggs but this, as well as the level of production, could certainly be improved.

North Holland Blue

North Holland Blues originated in Holland and are a heavy breed. They develop quickly into large birds reaching 10 lb. or more. Although a table breed, some strains are quite good layers. Regretfully the breed has lost its popularity which is a great pity for with its blue/grey barring and its slightly feathered legs both cock and hen are very handsome.

Indian Game

Valueless for commercial egg production, the Indian Game (*below*) is essentially a table breed. It has an exceptionally broad breast and is most often used for crossing with white-skinned table breeds such as the Light Sussex. The progeny make really superb table birds.
(Courtesy: *Understanding Indian Game*, K.J.G. Hawkey, *photo courtesy*: S.J.G. Jones)

POPULAR LIGHT BREEDS

The Leghorns

LEGHORNS came originally from the Mediterranean and, unlike the breeds mentioned earlier, they were always regarded as good layers. This light breed, which exists in more than ten different colours, was one of the main laying strains used in the poultry industry before hybrids were introduced.

The illustrations show Whites (*above*), Brown (*centre*), and Blacks (*below*).

Ancona

In all but colouring the Ancona is a very similar bird to the Leghorn. It was imported from Italy, probably some years before the latter, but has never achieved such popularity as, say, the White Leghorn. For a light breed it is comparatively hardy, however, and being a reasonable producer itself, some good egg-laying stock have resulted from Ancona–R.I.R. matings.

Minorca

Yet another breed which has fallen from grace, more through unwise breeding that from any fault of its own, is the Minorca. It was once valued as an excellent egg producer but there are few if any strains at present which can compete with the hybrids for commercial production. It is a fine-looking bird, however, and we would owe gratitude to whoever helped to re-establish it on profitable lines.

SOME USEFUL CROSS-MATINGS

Rhode Island Red–White Wyandotte

CROSS-BREEDING, provided it is done thoughtfully and correctly, can give a number of beneficial results. Its purpose, briefly, is to implant the good points of both parents in the progeny and for commercial purposes the system was widely used. The Rhode Island Red–White Wyandotte cross (*above*) was not so common but if Wyandottes of the right type were used, useful dual-purpose progeny would result. On the other hand, the Rholde Island Red – Light Sussex (*below*) was one of the most popular of all. The cockerels from the mating have white flesh of fine texture, while the pullets were noted as excellent egg-producers.

Rhode Island Red–Light Sussex

White Leghorn–Rhode Island

A further benefit of cross-breeding is the improved vigour which is noticeable in the progeny. "Hybrid-vigour", as it is called, is not just the result of wishful thinking on the breeders' part but is an acknowledged scientific fact which also has considerable commercial value. The White Leghorn–Rhode Island breeding pen (*above*) is a cross which was popular because the pullets gave an excellent account of themselves as layers. Crosses between light and heavy breeds combine something of the quick growth of the former with the steadier temperament of the latter, though the birds are only fair for table purposes. The Light Sussex–Rhode Island (*below*) was a useful table cross, the pullets as well as the cockerels being of value for this purpose.

These crosses have now become more "scientific" and hybrid strains have been developed, these replacing the popular crosses in the poultry industry. However, pure breeds or first crosses still have much to offer for the smallholder with free range. Hybrids are not really suitable for the fancier or small producer.

Light Sussex–Rhode Island

SEX LINKAGE

IT is a great advantage to the breeder if the appearance of his chicks makes it possible to determine their sex at hatching. To do this it is necessary to cross certain breeds (except in the case of the auto-sexing varieties) and, depending on the breeds employed, it is possible to distinguish between the pullets and the cockerels as soon as they are hatched either by their colouring, their markings or by the rate of feather growth.

White Leghorn

The most accurate of these methods is sexing by down colour. Chicks resulting from a cross between males with "gold" plumage and females with "silver" plumage will also have gold and silver down, but the colouring will be reversed. That is, the coloured chicks will be the pullets and the white chicks will be the cockerels.

The sex-linked cross illustrated on this page is that of a White Leghorn male with a Rhode Island female. In this case—a rapid-feathering male mated to a slow-feathering female— the sex can nearly always be told by the size of the wing feathers immediately after the chicks are hatched. In the female (*left*) these feathers are slightly longer, but the difference is very small and experience is needed for accurate sexing.

Rhode Island

White Leghorn–Rhode Island Chicks

Rhode Island Red   *Light Sussex*

Possibly the most popular and successful of all sex-linked crosses, the Rhode Island Red when mated to the Light Sussex gives very reliable results and there is no difficulty at all in distinguishing the gold pullets from the silver cockerels. Perhaps it should be made clear that sex-linkage does not work the other way round—silver male to gold female. All the chicks of a Light Sussex–Rhode Island mating (the male mentioned first) will be silver, irrespective of sex.

Rhode Island Red–Light Sussex Chicks

HYBRIDS

In recent years hybrid strains have become increasingly popular for both egg and table bird production. The best of these purpose-bred birds are capable of phenomenal performances in terms of egg output, speed of growth, low mortality rate, etc., whilst effecting great economy in feed conversion. Top picture shows trial breeding pens at one large specialised breeding farm.

Pictures above and on the left show typical hybrids developed for egg production. These are given either names or numbers by the large commercial concerns which originate and multiply them. Perhaps the biggest single advantage of hybrids over straight commercial first-crosses is their "repeatability". Bred from closed blood lines, they can be bred in unlimited quantities with very little variation. New factors can be introduced as and when required.

What's Your Market?

Pure-bred, cross-bred or hybrid? It's one of the first questions facing anyone taking up poultry-keeping, whatever the scale. And the answer rests largely with the purpose for which the birds are to be kept and, in the case of eggs, the proposed marketing outlet.

For intensive, commercial egg production, when the market is such that coloured shells will bring no price premium, hybrid stock are likely to prove most profitable. The view is supported by the results of numerous impartial trials and by achievements in commercial practice. But for at-the-gate sales, where tinted or brown shells are certain to be in demand, and a heavier egg is likely to be most popular, pure breeds or first-crosses may be the best bet. Even so, there are several hybrid strains where tinted shells are combined with a high rate of production.

Retail Sales

Retail sales at the farm gate have reached very considerable proportions of late, mainly where relatively small flocks are kept. Most producers selling this way fix their prices at 10 p or more per dozen above the official packing station price. Some have developed egg rounds in nearby residential neighbourhoods. To save both the customers' and the vendor's time it is now a common practice to display the eggs on a help-yourself stall or to use a vending machine.

INCUBATION–
NATURAL AND ARTIFICIAL

Egg Selection and Storage

NOT every egg is suitable for incubation. Reject eggs which are either below or above standard size (2 oz. to 2½ oz.) for by setting the former you will be tending to perpetuate the failing in future stock, while the over-large eggs often give unsatisfactory hatching results. Thin-shelled eggs should also be rejected.

Storing

For top hatchability eggs should not be stored for more than eight days prior to incubation. Eggs should be stored with pointed ends downwards, the ideal temperature of the storage room being about 50°F. Hatching eggs must be clean. Gentle wiping with a damp cloth is permissible but it is much better not to allow the eggs to get dirty in the first place.

Natural Incubation

Provided the hen is really broody, natural incubation is the simplest way of hatching small numbers of eggs. Management is confined to letting the hen off the nest for up to 20 minutes daily, during which time she will feed, drink and take a dust-bath. A hen will cover from 12 to 15 eggs.

The Nest Box

The nest box, or coop, should be 16 ins. square and have a solid wooden floor to keep out rats. A board should cover the front at night for the same reason but this must have liberal air holes along the top (*centre picture*). In hot weather the whole coop should be placed in the shade: it is useless simply to hang a sack over the front for this makes the interior stuffier than ever. Soft hay makes the best nesting material and should be supplied liberally when the hen is first put to sit. Put turf or earth round the edge of the box to make a saucer-shaped nest.

Nesting Precautions

Dust the hen thoroughly with insect powder before putting her on the nest and also scatter a little on the nesting material. As a further precaution, sprinkle a little in the spot she favours for a dust bath. On no account disturb the hen whilst the eggs are hatching. She will manage without food quite well for 48 hours.

Artificial Incubation

Most small poultry-keepers buy day-old or growing chicks to provide replacement stock. Even so, there are still those who prefer to do their own hatching for the added interest this provides, quite apart from small-scale breeders who, of course, hatch their own stock.

One or two firms still offer small incubators—either electrically or oil-heated—but it is also easy to purchase very cheaply older, discarded incubators still capable of useful service. Before use, carry out the maintenance procedure given on p. 54. Such an incubator may be either of the hot air or the hot water type but both sorts employ the same system of heat regulation. In oil-heated models, the flow of warm air into the incubator from the externally-mounted lamp is regulated by the expansion or contraction of a capsule situated above the eggs and connected to the damper by rods.

Incubators must be housed in a building not subject to sudden drastic temperature changes. Picture on the right shows a small electric incubator which has a transparent lid to give full visibility at all times.

Electric Incubator

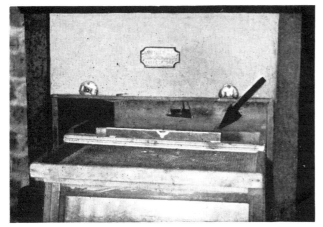

Must be Level

When preparing an incubator for use it is important to see that it is perfectly level. It is difficult to judge this accurately by eye and the surest means is to use a spirit level. It can be seen in this photograph resting on the partly-withdrawn tray.

Test the Thermometer

Much reliance is placed on the thermometer during incubation and it should be tested before each hatch. Simplest method is to compare the reading with that of a clinical thermometer when both are placed in water heated to 103°.

Between each hatching the incubator should be thoroughly cleaned and disinfected. This should also be done after the final hatch of the season. After the machine has been opened up and the fittings removed, these should be washed in a solution of washing soda (a generous handful to a gallon of water) and the interior of the machine washed or sprayed with a similar solution. Should chicks from the previous hatch have developed B.W.D., fumigation with formaldehyde gas will be necessary. A dish containing 2 oz. permanganate of potash is placed on the

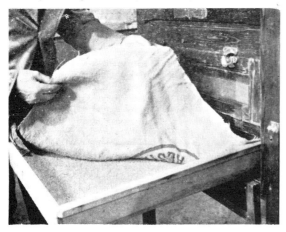

incubator tray. On to this is poured 1 oz. of commercial formalin. Close the machine and leave for four hours, taking care not to inhale the fumes. Cover all air outlets.

New Lining

The lining of the chick draw (*left*) should be replaced after each hatch, or every other hatch, with clean, fine sacking or hessian.

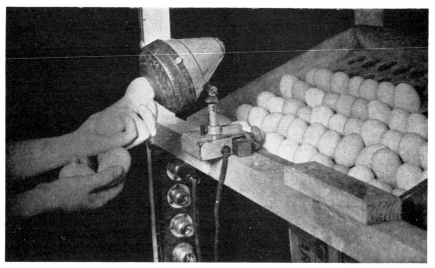

Egg Testing and Candling Lamp

It is best to test eggs twice during incubation so that infertile eggs, and those with dead germs, can be removed. A special candling lamp is useful but a powerful torch is quite satisfactory in a darkened room. The first test is made after a week and the second after a fortnight. Do not keep the eggs out of the incubator longer than is necessary. The job is best carried out in place of the routine turnings.

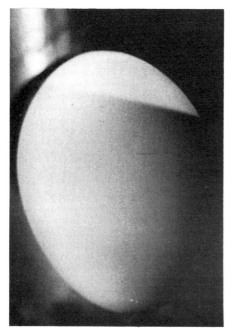

Infertile eggs, which should all be removed at the first candling, will appear practically the same as new laid eggs wheras the living embryo in fertile eggs shows as a distinct blob, from which radiate thin veins. Occasionally a red ring may be observed, this denoting a fertile egg in which the embryo has died soon after starting to develop.

Second Candling

Apart from the air space at one end, a 'living' egg will be uniformly dark when the second candling is carried out. Should the embryo have died during the second week of incubation, the air space will be less distinct.

Hen egg on the 16th day
(*Courtesy*: Dr. A.F. Anderson Brown)

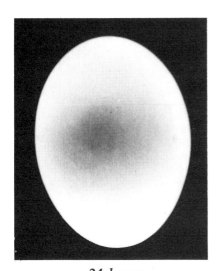

24 hours

The blastodisc is just visible.

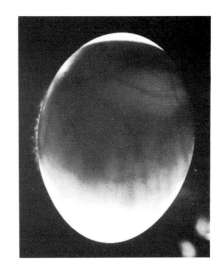

Eighth day

Considerable growth of the allantois obscures the embryo.

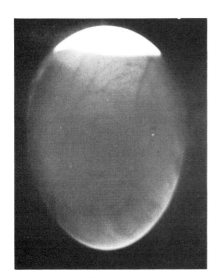

Tenth day

The allantois has now reached the small end of the egg, but only on the upper surface.

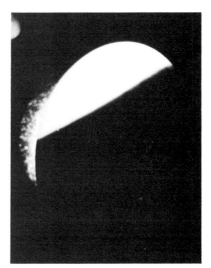

Nineteenth day

Completely blacked out. Will soon be ready to hatch.

(*Courtesy*: Dr. A.F. Anderson Brown – *The Incubation Book*)

Stages of Growth

Eggs should be checked and candled at the end of each week. Clears can be removed after seven days and those not developing can be discarded from seven to fourteen days (see next page).

Thermometer Readings

The bulb of the thermometer should never rest on the eggs but should be suspended about ¼ in. above them. A temperature of 103° F. is recommended for the first fortnight of incubation, reducing this by one degree for the remaining period. Hot-water machines have two thermometers, one showing the temperature of the water and the other the temperature in the egg draw (*top photo*). Hot air machines have a single thermometer, suspended from the roof of the egg compartment (*centre photo*).

Moisture of Air

Maintenance of an even and correct temperature throughout the 21 days of incubation is all-important for good hatching results but another factor to be taken into consideration is the humidity or moisture of the air in the incubator. Just how the air is kept moist will depend on the make and type of machine but a satisfactory atmosphere will generally be obtained by following the particular manufacturer's instructions. In some of the larger machines a hygrometer is fitted, this showing the percentage humidity of the atmosphere. Ideally it should be maintained at 60% (*right*).

Regular Turning

Throughout the incubation period eggs have to be turned two or more times daily to prevent the growing embryo from sticking to the outer membrane. This is a most important task and needs to be done with care. Each side of the egg should be marked —one side with a cross and the other with a circle—so as to make turning quicker and more accurate.

When eggs are incubated by natural means the hen turns them every hour with her beak, but such frequent turning has not been found necessary to get good results from an incubator. Indeed, when small machines are used it is often not advisable to turn them more than twice daily because of the cooling which must take place each time the eggs are taken from the incubator. Turning should be stopped three days before the eggs are due to hatch.

When machines are equipped with devices for turning eggs it is generally recommended that this be done four or five times daily. It has been said that this more frequent turning increases the final hatching rate by as much as 10%.

REARING STURDY CHICKS

Hen-Reared Chicks
the Easiest

IF a broody hen has hatched out the chicks herself she will invariably take to them without any trouble, but day-old chicks purchased from elsewhere, or hatched in your own incubator, must be introduced with a little care. This is best done at dusk, gently sliding each chick under at intervals of a few moments. Needless to say, the broody hen should have been tested first for several days on pot eggs. Hen-reared chicks are the least trouble and so long as the broody is reliable there is little to go wrong, especially if they have access to short clean grass.

Rearing Coop

Rearing coops should be about 2 ft. square and some 20 in. high, sloping to the rear. The bars across the front should allow the chicks to move in and out freely, the centre slats being removable to allow the hen out daily for exercise. Vermin must be kept out at night with a boarded front (don't forget the ventilation holes) while the floor can be covered with sand, dry earth or shavings, these being cleaned out and renewed each day. The coop and run (*see next page*) should be moved to fresh ground at the same time. A useful size for the run is 2 ft. wide and 5 ft. long.

Prevent Chicks Straying

In warm weather the chicks will leave the coop for short excursions right from the start and a run must be provided to prevent them from straying. The hen should be kept in the coop during the first fortnight and after this the run can be dispensed with and both hen and chicks allowed out together in a wire-netting enclosure.

The chick trough and water fount should at first be placed on a board just outside the coop. Feeding is as for artificially-reared chicks (*see page 63*) and water and food for the broody can be placed on the top of the run. Make sure that there is no gap or crack where the chicks can stray or get crushed—a frequent cause of losses.

Feeding and Watering

Keep Them Warm

The main need of newly-hatched chicks is warmth; they must not be allowed to chill whilst being moved to the brooder. Chicks sent by rail must be put in the already-warm brooder directly on arrival.

Brooding appliances are numerous, the brooder below being designed for intensive (indoor) rearing. A wire-netting surround is used to keep the chicks near the hover for the first few days but this is gradually extended.

Oil-heated Brooder

Hay Box Brooders

The hay, packed loosely between the outer walls and the circle of netting, retains the natural warmth of the chicks. No other heat is provided, though a 4 ft. run should be added to the outside. Sound chicks can be reared in this way but the chicks can be let out of the brooder only at feeding times for the first week.

Another home-made brooder is seen on the right, electric light bulbs, suitably protected, being the source of heat. Such devices should be well tested with a thermometer before use. Infra-red brooding (*below*) is a very simple method of intensive rearing. The chicks are under observation the whole time and the heat adjusted by raising or lowering the lamps. A 250-watt lamp is sufficient for up to 100 chicks.

Electric Lamp Brooder

Brooding with Infra-red Lamps

Sun Parlours

During the warmer months, outdoor brooders are ideal, providing the land used has not carried poultry for some time. Should this be impossible, sun parlours (*above*) are a useful compromise which allow sunshine and fresh air without the risk of infection.

Two Popular Outdoor Brooding Arrangements

The most important point to ensure when building or purchasing is that the brooder has sufficient insulation and reserve of heat to keep up the required temperature during cold spells.

Right Height For Lamps

Infra-red lamps are generally suspended 15–16 in. above the floor litter. The exact height should be determined by the behaviour of the chicks. All is well if they settle in a hollow circle around the perimiter of the heated area (*right*). Always provide a surround (cardboard or hardboard will do) for the first stage of brooding, extending it daily. A circle 4–5 ft. across will suit 100 day-olds. If a hover is used for rearing, the first week temperature should be a little over 90 deg. F. (two inches above the floor and mid-way between the heater and the outside wall) thereafter decreasing it by 5 deg. weekly until the chicks do without artificial heat at about six weeks.

Feeding Space

Ample feeding space must be provided, otherwise some of the birds may not get their fair share. Double the trough space should have been allowed in the centre photo.

Most chick rearers now feed either proprietary mash or crumbs. These are fed *ad lib* in hoppers or troughs. If the feed is given in open pans or on newspapers for a start it will encourage the chicks to begin feeding at the earliest possible moment.

A Good Start

The lower picture shows a simple but satisfactory set-up for the smaller rearer using an infra-red lamp. Points to note are the surround, clean floor litter, fully accessible feed, and water founts made from tins inverted over saucers. Lower ends of the tins have been nicked to allow the water to flow.

Hay Box Fold

The chick capacity which manufacturers claim for their brooders is generally based on their size at day-old. There will be room for only half as many birds when they are six weeks old. It follows that either the brooders can never be fully stocked or else some chicks must be removed during the brooding period. The hay-box fold, shown above, is one means of housing chicks which have got past the initial brooding stage and can manage with rather less heat. The roof of the covered portion is lined with hay, the amount being lessened as the chicks grow. Such folds are suitable for chicks 3–4 weeks old.

The range of brooder houses seen below allow the birds on to grass at an early age whilst giving good protection in case of bad weather.

Brooder Houses

At from six to eight weeks, depending on the birds' feather growth and the time of year, the brooder can be dispensed with altogether. If possible, the growing stock should then be moved to range houses or night arks. The latter type of housing, which can hardly be bettered for this purpose, is seen below. It has a slatted floor and is easily moved to fresh ground. During the warmer months only the wire-netting door should be closed at night.

Night Light

It is a good plan, especially in doubtful weather, to hang a hurricane lamp inside the ark for the first few nights. This will keep the temperature up and also help to prevent the birds crowding in the corners.

Outside Protection

Similarly, a few straw bales or wattle hurdles placed outside the ark will give the young birds some measure of protection from strong winds. The standard 6 ft. × 3 ft. ark will hold fifty or more six-week chicks but, as the birds grow, this figure should be reduced until there are no more than 25 birds in the ark when the time comes for them to be moved to their laying quarters.

Night Ark

Intensive Rearing

Pullets reared in confinement are every bit as good as those reared on range, providing a suitably balanced mash is fed. Intensive rearing saves a good deal of labour and growth is often more even. The growers in the house above have access to a wire-floored veranda. This makes it possible to stock the house more heavily (by about a third) and also provides occupation and fresh air.

Essentially a summer house for use in less exposed districts, the range shelter is an American idea which soon caught on in this country. Such housing (*below*) is cheap and it does rear healthy birds in any average summer. Shelters are easily made from rough timber but whether this is done, or one bought, see that it is light enough to be moved fairly easily.

Range Shelter

SEPARATING THE SEXES

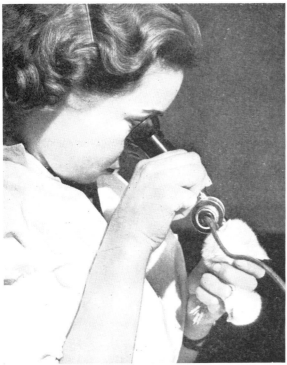

Sexing Machine

UNLESS he uses a sex-linked cross, the sexing of day-old chicks is too complex a task for the average poultry farmer. He must, therefore, rear the pullets and cockerels together for a start. until they reach an age when sexing is simple.

But though vent sexing at day-old normally takes several years to learn efficiently, there are now available sexing machines (*left*) which can be used accurately for day-old sexing after only a little training. When proficient, a farmer can sex many hundreds of chicks an hour. The relatively high cost of the machine is well justified on farms where surplus cockerels present a problem each year.

The sex of light breed chicks can be determined when they are about six weeks of age, whereas heavy breed chicks are difficult to judge before the two month stage, or even a fortnight later if you are inexperienced. Separate the sexes as soon as possible.

The earlier development of the male's comb and wattles shows clearly in this pair of light-breed chicks. The males are also leggier and are more quarrelsome than the pullets.

Sexing Light-Breed Chicks

Sexing Heavy-Breed Chicks

This is the earliest stage at which heavy-breed chicks can be separated with reasonable accuracy. The main contrast here is in feather growth, the male being sparsely feathered (*left*) and having little or no tail. The whole appearance of the male bird is coarser and more thick-set than that of the pullet and by eight weeks his voice will be noticeably deeper. By contrast, the young pullets appear more delicately made—particularly their heads and legs. By ten weeks the cockerels' combs will be conspicuously larger than those of the pullets.

Growth Contrast

This photo shows the contrast in heavy- and light-breed males of the same age. The heavy bird is on the left and is distinguished by his slow feather growth and lack of headgear and tail. The light bird, on the other hand, is nicely feathered and looks more like the miniature of an adult cockerel.

When separated, the cockerels are usually run on for the table market. If any are required for breeding the most likely specimens should be picked out at this stage and kept apart for final selection later on.

Contrast in Heavy- and Light-Breed Males

CULLING AT ALL STAGES

Is It Worth While?

The value of culling (removal of unsatisfactory stock) has become a matter of some controversy. In very large egg production plants it is often considered uneconomic, except for the disposal of obviously sick birds. But in the smaller unit it is still a factor of considerable importance. Whether it takes the form of individual handling or close visual observation depends on the numbers kept.

Spotting Culls

Spotting culls is a job which the experienced poultryman does almost by instinct. One soon learns, for instance, when a chick is not all that it should be. Even without handling, there is an air of vitality and well-being about the sound ones which will not be seen in weakly chicks. The good ones are soft and plump and full of life whereas the others may feel a little sticky and their movements will not be strong. *Cull all abnormal and weakly chicks as no amount of care will turn them into healthy ones.*

Contrasting Chicks

The chick in the top picture has been allowed to grow out of the day-old stage but will clearly never

be any good. The one in the centre is being examined for pasting round the vent which may denote B.W.D. (*see pp.* 131 *and* 132). An obvious contrast in health is seen at left.

Thorough Check-up

Though poorly chicks should be removed when-ever spotted during the weeks of brooding, the move from brooder to ark offers an excellent opportunity for a more thorough check up. If an otherwise healthy bird is just a little backward in feathering (*right*) it may pay to transfer it to another batch a week or so younger, but make sure that it handles satisfactorily. Such stock must not be retained for breeding, of course.

Typical Weaning-stage Culls

Note the awkward stance and long beak of the bird on the left and the general hope-lessness of the other specimen.

Chicks Suffering from Rickets

Chicks in the above photo are suffering from rickets, a deficiency disease confined mainly to young birds. The trouble could have been prevented by the inclusion of cod-liver oil in the mash. Rickets is often referred to loosely as "leg weakness". (*See also page* 143).

Promising Pullet

This pullet is just about ready to be taken from the rearing house and put into laying quarters. This is another important culling stage for there will be no room or food to spare for birds which lay indifferently. However, she clearly passes the test on external appearance (note the tight feathering and alert stance) and should be handled to see whether she has the necessary well-fleshed frame of good width and depth.

Signs of Health

The centre photograph shows a sound growing chicken bearing the obvious stamp of health. Note the upright carriage, good body depth, deep skull and large, bold eye.

Poor Specimen

The lower picture shows a bird which is the reverse of everything one looks for in a growing pullet and will clearly be of no use whatever. Apart from being a menace to her companions in that she is likely to be the first to contract any poultry disease going and may spread it to the others, she has already cost anything up to a pound to bring to this stage. Even as a table bird she is practically useless so the expenditure is not likely to be recovered.

No poultryman likes to get rid of a bird without good cause, but as a rule he will be well advised to market borderline cases before they slip back even further in condition. Always remember that it is the *average* output of a flock which determines its profitability.

Is She Laying ?

A reliable guide as to whether or not a bird is in lay may be obtained by handling it to feel (*a*) the distance between the pelvic bones and (*b*) the distance between the end of the breast bone and the pelvic bones. The former test is being carried out above. Space for only two fingers suggests that the bird is out of lay, but the bird on the right is in full production.

The second test, for capacity, is being carried out in the lower left-hand photo. There is space for four fingers between the pelvic bones and the end of the breast bone, a sign that the bird is laying well. A large, moist vent (*right*) is another sign that a bird is in full production. In non-layers the vent is dry and very much smaller.

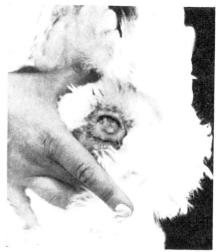

Good Layers

The Head

Much can be told from a fowl's head. All the heads shown on this page belong to poor specimens which should certainly be culled if handling confirms the bad impression they give.

The Eye

Note in each case the dull, sunken eye. They lack that bold look of vitality present in the head of a good layer. See how each head tapers at the front, instead of being rounded.

The Headgear

In each case it is shrivelled, a sure sign that the bird is out of lay, or laying only spasmodically. It should be borne in mind, however, that even good producers will have shrunken headgear when in the moult and so this point must be considered in conjunction with the general shape of the head and condition of the bird.

The Beak

Long and ugly, they are a sign that their owners are not used to scratching and pecking for their living and are yet another indication that they are a liability to the flock.

Good Producers

These are the heads of the flock's best layers—bright, prominent eyes; comb and wattles of good size and colour; the depth of the head carried well forward; short, business-like beaks. If you watch them at the food trough they always have a good appetite and they are amongst the first off the perch in the morning and the last to return at night. At the end of the laying season their feathering will be worn but they will retain their alert, active disposition until they moult. The legs and beaks of birds in which these parts are usually yellow will become bleached as the season advances.

Moult as a Guide

Heavy producers moult late, the poorer birds dropping their feathers weeks, or even months, earlier. And besides moulting late they usually get through this time of non-production (though a few birds do lay during the moult) without too much delay. A bird starting its moult in July or early August is seldom worth keeping for another season. Judge borderline cases on their other merits.

Catching Crate

A limited amount of culling can be carried out at night when the birds are on the perches, but catching crates are still used on some farms. Dimensions are 6 ft. × 3 ft. and the system of shutters and traps is easily seen. The birds should be driven from inside the house straight into the crate placed outside the pophole.

Culling Procedure

It is helpful to have two people engaged on culling—one for handling the stock and the other for making such notes as may be necessary, especially if the birds are under consideration for breeding. When driving the birds, and later handling them, be calm and quiet in your movements as a sudden panic amongst laying birds may do a great deal of harm.

What to Look For

The points mentioned on the previous pages should all be considered when a bird is taken from the catching crate. Note her health and vitality first, the condition of her headgear and feathering, and then handle her to judge body size, fatness, capacity, etc. Feel her skin: it should be soft and pliable, not coarse and tight.

KEEP THE PULLETS GROWING

Intensive Rearing

Pullets reared intensively must not be overcrowded. Not less than 3 sq. ft. per bird should be allowed for small flocks. See that they have adequate ventilation, without draughts, and feed them with dry mash, *ad lib*, as a precaution against boredom.

Free Range

Ideal for growing pullets (*centre photo*) so long as the land is not sour or poultry sick. Feed a balanced growers mash, with ample clean water at all times. Feeding with dry mash is labour-saving and provides the birds with occupation (*below*).

Parasites

Keep the stock free from parasites by sprinkling insect powder in their dust baths and inspecting the house and perches regularly for red-mite. See that nothing is holding up the birds' natural development.

FOODS AND FOOD PREPARATION

Use of Scraps

Domestic poultry-keepers, with only half a dozen or so laying pullets, are able to make use of house scraps and stale bread to eke out bought meal. It is also worth while purchasing fish scraps as these are an excellent source of protein and minerals. After cooking, all these scraps should be minced and mixed and then dried off with meal.

Mash Feed

The first mash feed should be given as early as possible in the morning, say 7.30 or 8.0 a.m., and the last feed about an hour before the birds go to roost in the winter, or at about 7.30 p.m. in the summer. Give grain at mid-day. Poultry-keepers who are not at home during the day should feed dry mash, ad. lib., in waste-proof hoppers. Tubular feeders (centre picture) are ideal.

Food Chopper

A number of food choppers are now marketed and these are particularly useful where potatoes form part of the feed. These and other scraps are chopped and mixed first and the meal is then added and the process repeated. The tool should be cleaned after use as it will otherwise clog with sour, stale mash. On no account should mash left from one feed be served up again. Meal fed with scraps should be a high-protein balancer type, scraps usually being low in portein.

Preparing the Mash

If your mash is too dry, as in the top photo, you will have difficulty in pressing it into a lump. If you feed a mash of this consistency you will find the wastage heavy and the birds will pick out the choicest pieces of food, leaving the rest.

Centre photo shows a sloppy, unpalatable mash which will not be eaten unless the birds are very hungry and have no choice.

Too Dry

Mixing a wet mash to the right consistency is soon learned. The lower photograph shows the ideal, a moist but crumbly mash which is neither too dry nor too soggy. Experience will soon tell you when the mash is in this desirable state but a simple test is to press a handful together, quite lightly, and then to drop the ball of mash from a height of about a foot. It should break back roughly into its original state.

Too Wet

The way to arrive at the ideal consistency is to keep the mash on the dry side until all the ingredients have been thoroughly mixed and then to add water to bring it up to the correct texture. A warm mash is greatly appreciated during the winter, especially for the first feed on cold mornings, so it is a good idea to add warm water when extra moisture is required. Never mix the mash overnight for use the next morning.

Feeding times provide the best opportunities for a quick daily check on the birds' health, for lack of interest in the food on the part of an individual bird is generally a sign that all is not well.

Just Right

Feeding Greenstuff

Greenstuff and Minerals

Greenfoods contain minerals essential to health, so do try to give birds of all ages a daily ration of something green—if your birds are fed largely on household scraps.

If you feed greenstuffs, and know there is a good proportion of animal protein in the ration (fish meal, meat meal, milk products, etc.,) there is probably no need to feed a mineral supplement, but where vegetable proteins are used to any extent it is a wise precaution to feed extra minerals. These can be purchased as a proprietary mix (*lower photo*) or a simple mixture can be made at home of equal parts of salt, steamed bone flour and ground limestone, this being fed in the mash at the rate of 2 per cent.

The quantity of food required by a laying pullet or hen depends largely on the type and quality of food which she is receiving. Thus, between 4 oz. and 5 oz. per day of a well-balanced, all-mash diet is generally sufficient, whereas 9 oz. or 10 oz. of food may be required by domestic layers if they are to extract the necessary nourishment from a diet consisting mainly of house scraps.

In any case, use measurements only as a rough guide when ordering supplies, etc. Always feed your birds according to what your observation of their behaviour and condition tells you, not according to the scales. When wet mash is fed, give them no more at a feed than they will clear up in half an hour.

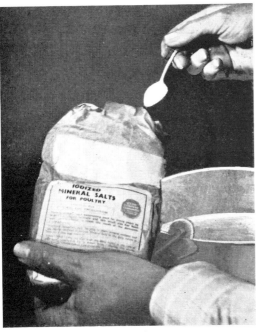

Mineral Mixture

Pellet Feeding

Pellets are simply dry mash which has been compressed into small cylindrical shapes. Very small pellets are compounded for young stock or, more frequently nowadays, irregular-shaped particles known as crumbs. The main value of pellet and crumb feeding lies in ensuring that the birds have a maximum intake of food. For chicks they can be fed *ad lib* in the sort of trough seen at right.

There are certain disadvantages, however. Appetites are soon satisfied with crumbs and pellets, leaving the birds with little occupation and the consequent danger of feather picking, etc. But for birds on range (*below*), especially during winter, they are an ideal concentrate.

Chick Trough

Self-Feed Hoppers

Dustbin Storage

Poultry foods are far too costly for there to be any excuse for wastage, but careless storage is more common than it should be. Dustbins make good rat-proof and weather-proof food containers and are especially useful for storing the rations for outlying stock. The lid of the bin seen here is attached to the handles with a long spring each side.

Meal stored in sacks in rat-proof sheds should be kept from contact with the concrete floor, where damp soon spoils both meal and bags. A slatted platform is easily made and should be built against a dry wall (*below*).

Slatted Platform

Some Points on Feeding

Poultry require different quantities of the various nutrients at different stages in their lives and according to the particular aim in view. Thus, chicks require substantially more protein during their first weeks than they do during the later growing stages. Pullets reared on grass of good quality will thrive when the protein content of the mash is comparatively low.

Nowadays, most poultry-keepers buy proprietary mashes which have been blended and balanced to fulfil a particular purpose. Provided a reputable brand is purchased, they offer a near-enough foolproof way of ensuring that one's birds are getting a correctly-balanced diet.

(*continued on next page*)

Drinking Water

For stock of all ages, a constant supply of clean water is absolutely essential. Twenty laying pullets need at least a gallon daily. A similar quantity is required by about 100 day-old chicks.

But these figures are very variable and water must never be rationed. On practically all commercial poultry farms, water is nowadays piped to valve-controlled troughs or hanging drinkers (right). Extensive use is made of polythene piping—easily installed by unskilled labour and very flexible in operation. Compared with filling water troughs by hand, a piped supply soon pays for itself by the labour it saves.

Drinking water for chicks should be given in troughs or founts which will not allow the birds to get wet. Drinking space requirements increase rapidly and an automatic supply should be introduced after a week or two.

Automatic Drinker

Some Points on Feeding—*continued.*

This almost universal use of proprietary feeds is one of the major revolutions which we have seen in recent years. True, some poultry farmers still prefer to mix their own rations but this is a skilled job and is simply not worth while for the smaller poultry keeper who has to buy the straight ingredients in small quantities. This is because modern knowledge of nutrition has resulted in extremely complex rations containing numerous ingredients, many in minute quantities. Therefore, with the exception of garden poultry-keepers who still wish to use scraps (and even they should buy a proprietary balancer ration) home-mixing is not recommended for the smaller poultry unit. For maximum economy, sufficient feed should be bought to last for two or three weeks after each delivery. Dry, vermin-proof storage is, of course, essential.

But if feedingstuffs have become more complicated, the method of feeding them has grown a good deal simpler. Stock of all ages are now fed with dry mash, crumbs or pellets, very often *ad lib* So long as the correct grade of feed is given, and the containers provide ample space and prevent wastage, there is little more to bother about. And because the feed is dry, it is quite in order to give sufficient at one feed to last for several days.

(*Continued on next page*)

Left: For hen-yards and other sem-intensive units, water piping should be buried one foot under the ground.

Below: Drinkers in intensive houses, particularly on litter, should be as splash-proof as possible. Damp litter around the drinker leads to disease build-up and dirty eggs.

Some Points on Feeding—*continued.*

Some controversy centres around the choice of feed containers. This point is more important than it may seem because it can have a big influence on feed wastage. Though often undetected on deep litter, such waste is readily seen when feeders are placed over slatted or wire floors.

Tube feeders have come in for a good deal of criticism in this respect, though the trouble is very often accentuated by bad adjustment. The base of the pan should be level with the birds' backs.

Troughs should not be more than half filled and must have a "spinner" along their length to prevent birds perching on the edges.

(*Continued on next page*)

Splash-proof Drinker

Water Container for Intensive House

Some Points on Feeding—*continued.*

Grain, sometimes given as a scratch feed to provide interest and occupation, should be rationed to suit the composition of the mash. An excess of grain will unbalance the ration. Before feeding grain, therefore, check with your feed supplier.

All poultry require grit, of a size to suit their age, and this should be provided *ad lib* in a separate hopper.   For layers, about 20 per cent of the grit should be medium grade flint, the remainder being oyster shell and limestone grit of a similar grade.

Grit Box

POULTRY MANURE

POULTRY manure is an extremely valuable fertilizer, being particularly rich in nitrogen. When it is realized that a flock of 50 birds will give some 5 tons of manure a year, and that this weight will be greatly increased when the soiled litter is taken into account, it will be seen how necessary it is to use this by-product to best advantage.

Modern systems of mechanization (*above*) greatly ease the work of clearing out the strawyard. If this is done annually the manure should be stacked to allow further rotting or spread on the land and immediately ploughed under.

Manure from the garden unit is best incorporated with vegetable waste in the compost heap (*right*) where it will help to speed rotting.

Store under Cover

If at all possible, manure should be stored under cover. In this way the full value of the manure is retained instead of being washed away into the surrounding soil by rain. The picture shows that such protection can be given at little expense and the best plan is to stack the manure with alternate layers of soil or sand, turning it at least once to assist even rotting throughout.

MODERN "EGG FACTORIES"

THE present is a time of great change in the poultry industry. Though most egg producers still use the more conventional systems and management methods, there is a growing trend towards the larger, super-intensive unit of the type seen above. The pullets are kept either in multi-bird batteries, or on slatted or wire floors, and the environment is fully controlled.

Time Switch

Many of these houses are windowless. The artificial lighting is regulated by time switch (above) to provide the pattern most favourable to a high level of egg production. To get maximum benefit, replacement pullets must be reared intensively, too, so that they reach point-of-lay with a low level of lighting. Some laying houses are fitted with radio loudspeakers (right): this appears to keep the birds more docile. The treble aim in house design is to ensure maximum stocking capacity, to provide near-enough ideal conditions and to reduce labour requirements to the minimum.

Insulation

Good ventilation and a reasonable degree of insulation are essential when houses are stocked super-intensively—sometimes as heavily as one pullet per sq. ft. Though ventilation is the more critical, it is very difficult to avoid condensation, and to ensure a fairly even temperature, if the roof and walls are unlined.

Insulation may take the form of an interior lining of asbestos board or hardboard, with an air space left between the inner and outer skins. For greater efficiency, a layer of glass fibre may be laid in the cavity, or else a layer of reflective material such as aluminium foil. Unless the interior board has a moisture-proof surface, a vapour seal must be included to prevent moisture condensing on the lining. Joints between boards must be sealed, too.

Controlled Lighting Patterns

In houses with windows, a popular plan is to provide a 22-hour "day" for the first two weeks, then to reduce this by regular amounts to reach a natural day-length at 22 weeks. This level is maintained during the laying period, unless the natural day-length shortens. In this event, supplement with artificial lighting to maintain the level. After mid-summer, keep the day-length at 17 hours.

In windowless houses, a similar plan can be adopted, stepping down to 14 hours at 22 weeks. Alternatively, after providing 22 hours of light for the first two weeks you can step down the day-length by 70 minutes weekly to an 8-hour day at 14 weeks of age. Maintain this until the birds are 22 weeks old and then increase the day-length by 20 minutes weekly until a 14-hour day is reached. Keep at this until there are signs of production declining, then stimulate by stepping up again by 15–20 minutes weekly to a maximum of 18 hours.

Ventilation

Ventilation requirements depend on the number of birds in the house. In intensive units, an extraction capacity of 2 cu. ft. per minute is needed for every pound of bodyweight of the flock. Thus, 1,000 5-lb. pullets need an extraction capacity of 10,000 c.f.m. One 12-in. diameter cowl has an extraction rate of 283 c.f.m. Allow about 5 sq. in. of inlet space per bird.

Overhead-Rail Feed Barrow

Picture above shows the extraction shaft above an electric fan. A 12-in. fan, revolving at 900 r.p.m. has an extraction rate of 700 c.f.m. Picture on the left shows a baffled air intake in a poultry house wall.

Speedier Feeding

Feeding can take a disproportionate amount of time unless steps are taken to mechanise it. Top picture on this page shows a mono-rail feed carrier, with troughs placed conveniently alongside. In some bigger units, feeding is entirely automatic.

Picture on the right shows one method of rearing intensively. Chief advantages are savings in labour and space.

Nest Arrangement and Egg Collection

Egg collection, cleaning and packing are the jobs absorbing most labour in modern "egg factories". Much thought has been given, therefore, to ways of speeding these tasks. In battery units (below) it is now quite common practice to collect eggs only about twice a week. It is important to have floors of good length so that the birds cannot easily reach the eggs.

Rollaway nests, with sloping wire floors, are very popular now in slatted and wire floor houses. Both individual compartments and communal nests are used. They are generally sited alongside the service passageway. For pullets coming into lay it is generally advisable to straw the floors until the birds have come to accept them. For batteries there are now mechanical egg-collecting devices (*below*) though they are not yet used very widely.

GOOD STOCK — MORE PROFIT

Some Points on Breeding

BREEDING is essentially a job for the specialist but the small farmer can obtain satisfactory results if he pays really strict attention to selection and management. Prime essential in all breeding stock is vigour and good health, this being ascertained by observation and careful handling. Second to this, where the female bird is concerned, comes its performance in the nest box. Ideally, this is ascertained by trap nesting, the photographs showing indoor and outdoor nesting units.

Every Egg Recorded

Outdoor Nesting Unit

Not for Breeding

Selection of a first-class male for a breeding pen is of paramount importance. His vigour, type and breeding will be reflected in all the progeny. Selection may to some extent be based on his pedigree records but of equal or greater importance is a study of the bird's external characteristics, combined with handling.

The ideal stock bird is, above all, vigorous. He is generally aggressive on the least provocation—the undoubted "master of all he surveys". Handling should reveal a heavy body, of ample width and depth.

Much can be told from the headgear, which should be well developed and full of colour. Compare the sunken eye and shrivelled headgear of the cock in the top picture with the fine headgear of the stock cockerel below. The comb and wattles of the bird in the centre picture have been dubbed (removed) to prevent their being frost bitten. (*See page* 128.)

Comb and Wattles Removed

No attempt should be made to breed from a cockerel until it is fully matured as its growth is likely to receive a check and this, in turn, will be reflected by low fertility. As a rule, nine months is quite soon enough to start using a male for breeding, though well-grown, light breed cockerels may be used a month or so earlier if need be.

Stock Cockerel

Flock Mating

The number of hens which can be run with each male depends on the system of mating used and also on the breed concerned. When heavy breeds are flock-mated (*above*) the usual allowance is one male for up to 15 females: light breed males will manage rather more—15 to 20, or even one or two more. Flock-matings give the best results when the birds have plenty of room to range about in, and it has been found that a few straw bales, or other obstacles, placed in the pen, prevent disturbance by other males during the act of mating.

In pedigree work it is, of course, necessary to know the male parent of each chick. Individual breeding pens (*below*) must then be used. The same number of females advised above can make up the pen but it is possible to economize on the male birds if the females are kept rather fewer in number and a single, really vigorous male used in alternate pens on alternate days. If only a small run can be provided, the number of hens to each male bird should in any case be reduced.

Individual Breeding Pens

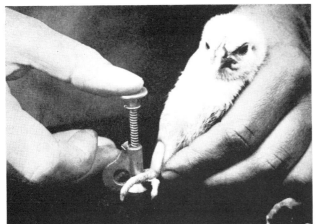

Toe-punching

A method of marking the chicks which is most commonly used on smaller farms. The number and positioning of the holes punched in the web between the toes gives a fool-proof record, providing the markings are carefully duplicated in the pedigree record book.

Pedigree Breeding

Pedigree breeding demands that the origin of the chicks be known without any shadow of doubt and this necessitates marking the eggs as they are taken from the trap nest and marking the resultant chicks as soon as they are hatched. To avoid confusion at hatching time, each hen's eggs are put together in muslin hatching bags at the time of final candling Throughout this work, full written records, generally in chart form, must also be kept.

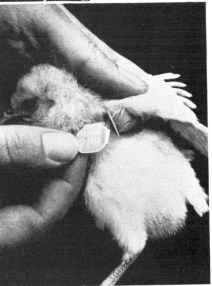

Wing Marking

Wing-bands and wing-tabs (*above*) are probably the most satisfactory method of all, it being a simple matter to fasten the bands securely in the loose skin of the wing. Each tab or band is numbered and there is no limitation to the method as with toe-punching.

Leg Rings

Leg rings work on the same principle but are now going out of favour as they must be replaced by larger rings as the chicks grow older (*left*).

EGG PRODUCTION IN WINTER

Windows and Raised Flooring

MERELY shutting the birds away in winter is not enough—they must have light, dry flooring and ventilation in fully intensive housing. The pullets in the top picture have excellent conditions, even though the house is very simple and inexpensive. Limited window space necessitates artificial lighting throughout a 14-hour day. Note the ample perch space and roomy feed containers.

An unprotected pophole can be a serious source of draughts in the semi-intensive unit: the litter and floor inside may become wet with driving rain. Photo shows one simple way of preventing the trouble (*also see page* 19) which can be easily removed during hot, airless weather to increase the ventilation.

Protected Pophole

Protected Runs

Alternate runs should be used for semi-intensive units as the ground will become a quagmire during prolonged wet weather unless given a rest. Note, too, how effective a wind-break is provided here by sheets of corrugated iron —a great inducement to winter laying.

Roofwork

Late summer is the best time for checking and repairing roofs and woodwork. If new felt is needed it will pay to buy a heavy grade of a well-known make. Lay it *across* the roof (not from ridge to eave) allowing generous overlapping at the edges and sealing the joints with the solution sold specially for the purpose. Before felting, the wood should be treated with wood preservative. If the old felt has not gone too far, a coating of bituminous paint may be sufficient.

Damp Nest Boxes

Outside nest boxes frequently become damp from water seeping down where the lid is hinged. A flap of roofing felt tacked along the wall of the house and bent to act as a gutter will remedy the trouble. The whole house should be treated regularly with creosote or a proprietary wood preservative.

Adequate Ventilation

This is essential to health: in deep litter houses, too, it must be up to standard if the litter is to "work" properly and retain its texture. Light (not necessarily direct sunlight), is likewise essential for health and production. Intensive houses are best ventilated by a system of extractor cowls and baffled air inlets, but hopper type windows and ridge caps are very widely used still. There should still be some provision for ventilation (*top photo*) even when the windows have to be closed in severe weather.

Insulate the Windows

Good insulation is a great aid to winter egg production (see p. 87) and is almost essential when houses are heavily stocked on the wire or slatted floor systems. When insulating an older-type poultry house, do not forget the windows, which often occupy a considerable proportion of the wall area. Easiest way to double-glaze windows is to secure plastic sheeting in place by means of battens.

Air Inlet

A sliding glass panel is a common form of air inlet. Note the small mesh wire netting to prevent vermin getting in. A baffle should be fastened inside to prevent draughts across the floor. If the air inlets are made under the droppings board this will keep the birds from direct draughts at night.

Greenfood

Fed in racks or hoppers, it serves a number of purposes. Most important, it provides occupation and interest for intensively-housed layers and so helps prevent vices beginning. Don't be discouraged if the birds mostly ignore it at first. They will soon learn to enjoy greenfood if it is fresh and clean. Another point is that greens will help to put right any small mineral deficiency there may be in the ration. Finally, the eggs from birds which have had regular supplies of greenfood have rich orange-yellow yolks. Cabbage, Kale, Brussels sprouts tops, etc., are all suitable. Sliced roots may be given if greens are scarce.

The birds peck at the greenfood through the 1 in. mesh netting in the hopper (*above*). Another popular method in domestic runs is to hang the greens from the roof (*bottom picture*) but don't put them much above the birds' reach as, contrary to popular belief, the jumping may do more harm than good. Never just throw the greens on to the litter; they will soon be unpalatable and will be left to rot.

Feeding Greens

Shelter for Runs

Provided they are dry under foot, poultry do not appear to mind cold weather in the least. Their bodies are too well insulated for it to have much effect. But they do need protection from strong winds—warm or cold. Egg production in semi-intensive units will soon suffer during windy weather unless protection is given (*top photo*). If the expense is prohibitive (though rammed straw walls are satisfactory) at least give shelter from prevailing winds.

The back-garden unit (*below*) is generally quite well sheltered but this often leads to damp or even muddy ground, especially if the birds have only a limited run. The answer is (*a*) to assist the natural drainage, if at all possible; (*b*) raise the house high enough for the fowls to take their dust bath beneath and (*c*) to provide sufficient inside scratching space for really bad weather. Very small runs should be covered, of course.

Back-Garden Unit

Garden Outing

Domestic layers, especially heavy breeds and crosses, kept in small houses and runs, greatly enjoy being let out into the garden for a few hours on a winter's day. They'll do little or no harm and will, in fact search for slugs and grubs once they get used to the idea. The interest and exercise, as well as the insects, are definite aids to egg production. Put them back in the run at feeding time.

Nest Box Design

A little thought to nest box design, and the litter provided, will encourage layers to use them in preference to the floor and odd corners. If of the individual type (*below*) suitable dimensions are 15 in. wide, 15 in. deep, 15 in. high in front and 25 in. high at the rear. Provide one box for every four or five pullets. Hay, straw or sawdust are suitable litters, the latter scoring on cleanliness and cheapness.

Artificial Light

Artificial lighting, used either before daylight or after sunset, encourages production during the time when natural daylength is shortest. Increased production will mean higher food consumption, however, so see that both feed and water are available.

Fourteen-hour Day

Lighting should be given to extend the fowls' day to 14 hours. If given at night, a dimming device will be required (otherwise the birds will be stranded when the light goes out) whereas in the morning a time switch is needed to turn the light on. Whichever is chosen, keep the times regular. Lighting has also been used in folds with success (*below*).

Lighting in Folds

Severe Weather

Crisp, dry snow will do no harm to the birds (though they may be reluctant to venture outside) but they are best kept in the house when it starts to thaw. So long as the roof is strong, a coating of snow will act as extra insulation from the wind. It is as well to brush the snow off the outside nest boxes otherwise water may eventually seep through when the snow melts. Brush the snow from the windows (*below*) as the interior will otherwise be darkened. Sweep away any snow which has found its way into the house itself.

Lamp Prevents Freezing

Birds in full lay require considerable quantities of water daily, especially if feeding on dry mash. If it is allowed to freeze they will have to go short and production will suffer at once. Exposed water containers can be kept from freezing if a small brooder lamp is placed underneath (*above*). Some form of lagging will help if heat cannot be provided.

Night Precaution

There is just room for a small Putnam lamp under this water vessel. Failing this, the water should be emptied out last thing on frosty evenings and the container filled with warm water first thing the following morning. If necessary, throw away ice and refill with warm water during the day.

MANAGEMENT IN SUMMER

Shade and Ventilation

Egg prices during the spring are generally lower than during the winter but production must be kept at the highest possible level if a satisfactory profit is to be obtained on the whole year's work. Points in warm-weather management are the provision of ample shade and ventilation, regular measures against insect parasites (*see p.* 148) and constant care against dirty and insanitary conditions which may lead to disease.

False Door

Small poultry houses, especially of the lean-to type, are very liable to become over-heated in hot weather. The flow of air can be increased by fixing a false door, made of strip wood and netting, inside the main doorway (*top photo*). In very hot weather, hay or pea haulm may be spread over the roof to assist insulation.

Keep Windows Open

Windows should be left open day and night. If they normally open only a little way, fit chains to hold them wide open (*centre photo*) wherever this is possible.

Birds on range may suffer from heat prostration unless shade is provided. It should be sufficient to cover the feed trough and drinking vessels. Ordinary range houses do not give enough shade if they are stocked with anywhere near the full complement.

Shade for Birds on Range

With the possible exception of point-of-lay pullets, all stock benefit from being folded or ranged on stubbles. Apart from the grain, insect life is abundant and adult birds will find the greater part of their own ration. Yearling birds being carried through the moult for a second laying season (*below*) will benefit most of all, coming in to lay again quickly and in fine condition.

Folds on the Stubble

Cleaning Routine

Left-over wet mash will very quickly go sour in hot weather and will attract flies. Scrub troughs and any other feeding utensils regularly with hot soda-water, rinsing them afterwards. The water container should also be cleaned out every few days. Before fresh water is given the receptacle should be emptied each time—not merely topped up. Place the vessel in the shade, as warm water is unpalatable and the birds will not drink sufficient.

EGGS–CLEANING

Combined egg basket and egg cleanser
(*Courtesy: Poultry World*)

Egg Collection

THE plastic coated basket is much more hygenic than the old type of wicker basket because it can be washed and sterilized regularly. In the example shown here, we see the eggs being placed in the egg cleansing machine after they have been collected.

Readers should note that under E.E.C. regulations there is a strict code of conduct regarding cleaning, and egg producers should be aware of the regulations operating at any particular time.

Collect Twice Daily

Most of the eggs will be laid in the morning and these should be collected when the midday feed is given. A further collection should be made after the evening feed. The extra labour of twice-daily collection is repaid by reduced breakages and lessening of egg-eating danger.

Change Nest Litter Frequently

Dirty eggs may be unavoidable from range or semi-intensive flocks during wet weather, but they should seldom occur in intensive houses. Check any tendency to the birds sleeping in the nests. Hay and straw are popular nest litters but sawdust is even better.

Site the nest boxes well away from the pop hole in semi-intensive houses and put clinkers or rubble just outside. A Danish idea is to put broad landing-ledges along the rows of nests. These have lipped edges and are sprinkled generously with chalk to dry and clean the birds' feet.

Clean Eggs

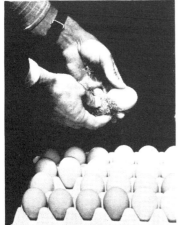

If eggs must be cleaned, keep them as dry as possible. Steel wool is excellent (*left*) though a damp rag may be needed in some cases. Never scrub the eggs under a running tap or, even worse, soak the dirt off in warm water. An emptied wet mash bucket is not a suitable receptacle for collecting eggs.

A number of efficient egg cleaning machines are now marketed and may be justified on larger plants. But it cannot be stressed too often that it is far better to produce eggs that do not *need* cleaning. It *can* be done and home-produced eggs would have a better name if more pains were taken in this direction.

Egg Cleaning Machine

What Candling May Show

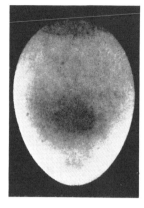

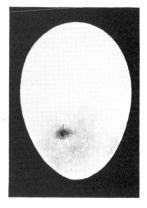

Fresh Egg

This is how an egg should look when held up to a powerful light. The yolk is only just visible and the air space (barely detectable here) is of moderate size.

Stale Egg

Generally has a larger air space. The yolk appears as a dense mass—much darker than the contents of a new laid egg.

Blood Spot

This, caused by the rupture of a tiny blood vessel, is easily seen. Such eggs are quite fit to eat but should not be marketed. They are most often produced by birds in full lay.

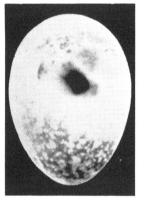

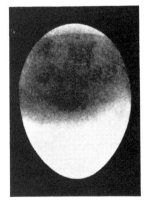

A "Hair" Crack

Air from outside has entered the air space of this egg, thereby enlarging it. These tiny cracks, not easily seen at a glance, occur most frequently in thinly shelled eggs.

Yolk Broken Free

This egg has been roughly handled at some stage as a result of which the yolk has broken free and is touching the shell. A mould, seen as a dark blob, has developed, making the egg unfit for human consumption.

Broken Yolk

The yolk is again touching the shell in this egg, but as a result of the yolk membrane breaking. Such an egg soon goes bad and is, of course, quite unfit for marketing or preserving.

EGG COLOUR

(Courtesy: Poultry World)

SOME breeds, such as Marans and Barnevelders (above) and Welsummers (below) lay deep brown eggs which are preferred by many customers. Other breeds; e.g. Leghorns, will lay more eggs, but these will be white and, therefore, not as attractive. Photographs are given earlier.

(Courtesy: Poultry World)

Selection of Breeds

1
2

Exhibition Types

Many exhibition breeds combine satisfactory laying ability and table qualities:
1. Old English Game
2. Rhode Island Red *(Courtesy: Poultry World)*

4

3

3. Light Sussex (Bantams)
   (Courtesy: Hall & Sons)
4. Light Brahma Pullet
   (Courtesy: R.D. Barnard)

It will be seen that beauty and utility can go together.

Broiler Production

The specialised broiler industry is able to produce ready-for-the-table fowl at an early age. View of intensive deep litter rearing (above) and prepared-for-the-oven broiler in special packaging for marketing and keeping in a deep freeze.

(Courtesy: Poultry World)

Retail Selling Again

As with egg production, the smaller producer of table poultry can often do best by developing retail sales. The extra money to be earned in this way will often more than compensate for the lack of discounts on feeding-stuffs, etc., which favour the big producer.

First step is to determine what class of bird is needed to meet local demand and then to set about producing it and processing it to ensure the really first-class product which is so essential for this class of trade.

Very likely, you will find that larger birds, such as capons, are the best line. Housing after the brooding stage can be quite simple, such as the ark-and-parlour set-up below, while feeding should be with chick mash for about 10 weeks, followed by growers' mash from then until marketing at up to 20 weeks of age.

Wet mashes may help to encourage appetites during the final weeks before killing when there is a danger that the birds may lose interest in their feed.

Sun Parlour is also Effective

Chemical Caponising

Chemical caponising (i.e. castration) is carried out with the aid of synthetic hormones about a month before killing. Purpose is to increase the final weight and to ensure a "soft", tender carcase. Pellets sold for this purpose are inserted with a special implanter.

Working in a sitting position, first grasp the birds legs firmly between your own. Then, pinching up the loose skin at the top of the neck, push the implanter firmly under the surface and eject the pellet. (*Centre picture.*) Finally, withdraw the implanter and with the other hand feel to make sure that the pellet has been inserted properly.

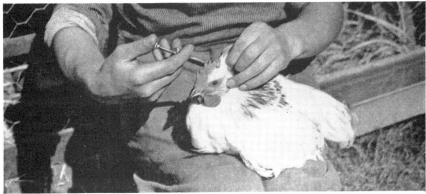

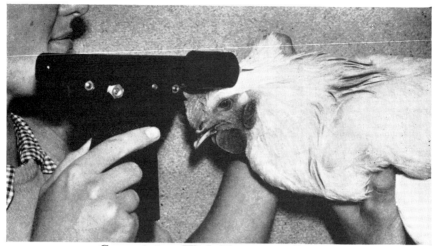

Caponising With Hormone Cream

An alternative to pellet implantation is the use of hormone cream. The special gun used for this purpose ejects just the right quantity of the cream. Whichever method is preferred, the instrument and needle should be absolutely clean. Also, the hands of the operator. After-effects are rare but the careless introduction of germs may obviously have harmful results. Work quickly and smoothly to reduce stress as much as possible.

Wax Plucking

In addition to the methods of plucking shown on the two fol-ing pages, wax plucking offers a means of achieving an excellent finish with very little skill or experience. After plucking the large wing and tail feathers from the freshly-killed bird, it is swilled to and fro for about 10 seconds in paraffin wax heated to 135 deg. F. Allow the surplus wax to drip back into the container, wait till the wax on the car-case becomes fairly hard and then strip it off, together with the feathers. Reclaim the wax by reheating and straining. An old wringer can be a help here. The container you use for wax should have a water jacket separating it from the source of heat.

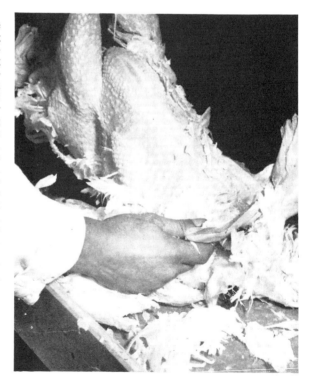

Killing and Plucking

Few people relish the task of killing an animal or bird. However, where poultry are concerned the task can be undertaken with confidence by anyone of normal strength. If preferred, there are several quite effective humane killers. Birds should be starved for 24 hours before being killed.

In the more usual method (*top left*) the bird's legs are grasped in the left hand and the right hand is allowed to slide along the neck until the head is grasped firmly in the palm of the hand, with the fingers under the throat. A firm pull downwards, combined with a backward thrust of the head, and the neck is dislocated. You will feel the neck "give" quite distinctly.

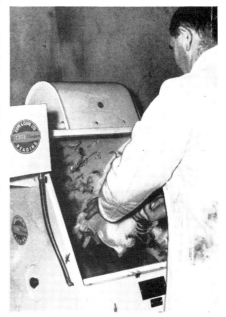

The flapping which follows is only a reflex action and the eyes will be seen to be closed. The photo (*top right*) speaks for itself, though warning must be given not to pull too hard otherwise the skin may be broken or the head be pulled right off.

On large plants it may pay to invest in a mechanical plucker (*right*). These machines are easily worked and make possible a far greater output even by unskilled labour.

Mechanical Plucker

The Breast

The Back

The Wings

Each bird should be plucked as soon as fluttering has ceased as the task is much easier while the carcase is still warm. A box or bath is needed to catch the feathers, and an apron should be worn.

Start with the breast (*top left*) then work round to the back (*right*) and finally to the wings and tail (*lower photo*). Grasp only a few feathers at a time and do not be in too much of a hurry until you have gained experience otherwise you will tear the flesh. It is helpful to keep the fingers moist. Pull the flight and tail feathers out singly.

Scald Method

Plucking is made very much quicker and easier if the bird is first immersed in water heated to 128 deg. F. for about 20 seconds. Swill backwards and forwards to make sure that the water reaches the skin all over. This should be done as soon as kicking has stopped after killing and plucking can proceed directly afterwards.

Use for Feathers

Feathers are a valuable by-product of poultry-keeping and are worth collecting for sale. Domestic poultry-keepers can use them in the home for making cushions, etc. The wing and tail feathers should be kept separately; also white feathers. About ¼ lb. of feathers is obtained from a bird of medium size.

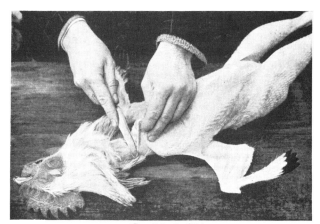

Cut Neck Skin

Dressing a Fowl

Table birds are normally sold dead and rough plucked. They are not drawn or trussed. However, many small producers like to build up a private trade in birds dressed ready for the table and most domestic poultry-keepers also like to prepare their own fowls.

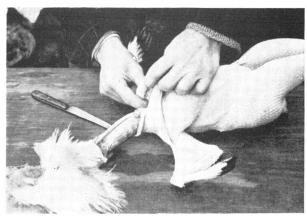

Loosen Neck

To prepare a bird for table, cut the neck skin an inch or so away from the body and then make a lengthways slit back towards the body. Do not remove the large flap of skin as this is needed to cover over the neck cavity later.

Remove Head and Neck

Insert the right forefinger under the skin and loosen the neck from the surrounding membranes. Then, using a clean, dry, cloth, remove the neck and head (*left*) with a firm pull. Make certain that the skin is not allowed to become blood-stained.

The Crop

The crop is easily removed when grasped with a dry cloth. Note how empty this one is on account of the bird having been starved for the correct time before killing. Insert your forefinger into the body again and loosen the lungs from the chest wall.

Leg Sinews

(1)

The next operation is to remove the leg sinews. Though not strictly necessary with very young birds it should always be done with older fowls, whether for roasting or boiling. Use a sharp knife to cut through the skin of each leg as shown in the centre photo. This will expose the sinews.

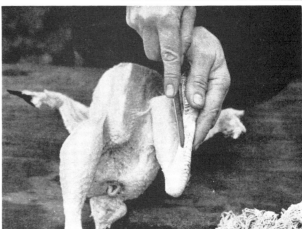

(2)

Insert a knife steel or skewer under the sinews of one leg and loosen them as far as possible. Make sure that you have gathered up all the sinews as they vary in size and it is possible to overlook one.

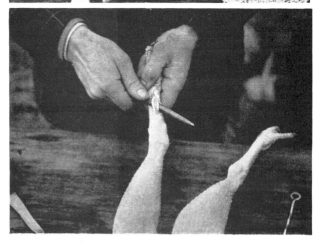

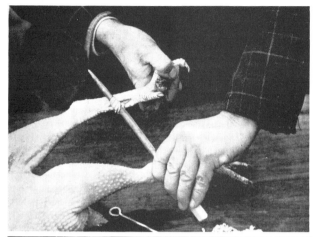

(3)

The steel is then given a twist. If the foot is held firmly with the other hand, so that the leg remains outstretched, further pressure on the steel will snap the sinews inside the leg.

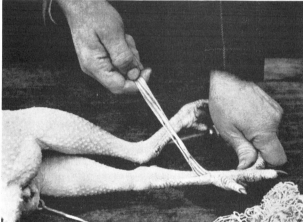

(4)

Once this has been done it is a simple matter to withdraw the sinews from the upper half of the leg. At no time is it necessary to grasp the fleshy part of the leg and any tendency to do this should be avoided as the skin is easily damaged.

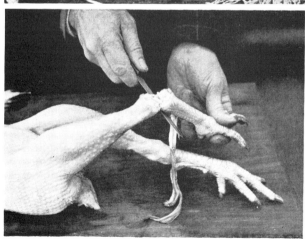

Removal of Leg

Finally, each leg is chopped through just below the hock. If no chopper is available, the skin surrounding the hock can be cut and the leg broken off at the joint (*left*) but there is a tendency in this case for the skin to shrink away from the knuckle during cooking.

Wing Tips

The tips of the wings are easily removed with a sharp knife when laid on a flat surface. Keep your hands clean throughout these operations, and wipe the table or board at frequent intervals, otherwise the skin may become stained or discoloured.

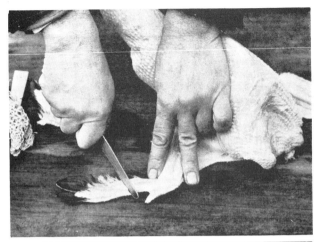

Horizontal Slit

Next, lay the bird on its breast and hold the tail stump, or parson's nose, in the left hand. The hole through which the bird's organs are extracted is begun by cutting a horizontal slit between the parson's nose and the vent, but taking care not to go so deeply as to cut the intestines. The vent can then be cut right out.

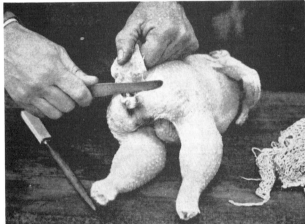

Loosen Organs

Insert your finger into the hole and gently loosen the organs within reach. This is not necessary with very young birds but older fowls, especially those which have grown over-fat, are not so easy to draw.

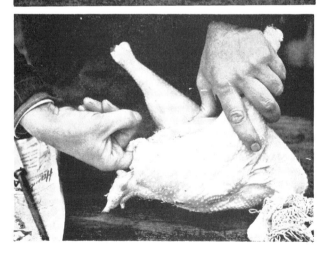

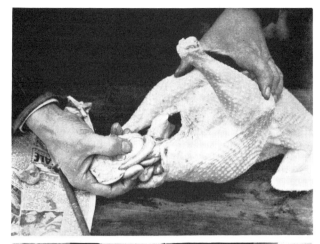

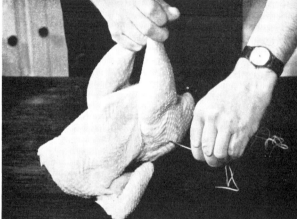

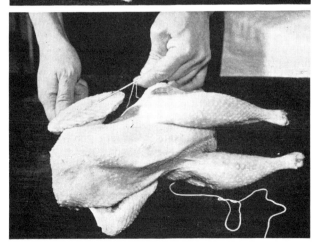

Amongst the soft organs will be felt a smooth object, somewhat larger than a golf ball, and flattened. This is the gizzard. If this is grasped firmly with the right hand, and the bird's body held with the left, the whole of the organs can be withdrawn at once. From these the heart, liver and gizzard should be removed. Together with the neck, they form the giblets. The gizzard is slit open and the contents and lining thrown away. The bluish-green gall bladder must be removed from the liver, taking care not to break it as the contents will give a bitter flavour to the flesh.

Trussing

To truss a bird for table, first place it on its back and lift up both legs. Thread the trussing needle through the lower part of the legs and through the body, leaving an equal amount of string each side (*centre photo*).

Next, turn the bird on its side and pass the needle through the fleshy part of the folded wing and then out through the wing tip. This should be done on each side (*lower photo*).

Cover Cavity

Surplus neck skin should then be drawn over the neck cavity. The wings should be folded back and across this surplus skin. The two ends of string protruding from the wing tips are drawn in, thus bringing the wings in tightly to the sides of the bird and across the surplus skin, holding this in place firmly.

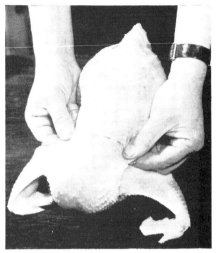

Cooking Reminders

For Roast Chicken: Stuff the neck end with forcemeat and put a little dripping in the body—also an onion, if liked. Cover the breast with fat bacon. Put the bird in a hot oven and baste at intervals. Remove the bacon ten minutes before the bird is ready. Temperature should be 450° (Regulo Mark 7) and, depending on the age, from 45 minutes to about $1\frac{1}{2}$ hours is needed for cooking.

*

To roast an older fowl, prepare as for chicken but being generous with dripping and bacon unless the bird is naturally fat. Place breast *downwards* in the baking tin (also containing dripping) and cover with another inverted tin. Cook *very* slowly in a gentle oven, removing upper tin and bacon a short while before the fowl is ready.

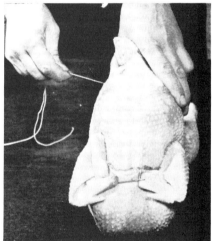

Secure Legs

To secure the legs in position, pass the needle through the back of the bird and just below the tail—

—turn the bird over and push the needle through the flesh just under the breast bone. Each end of the string should pass through this spot, though in different directions, of course.

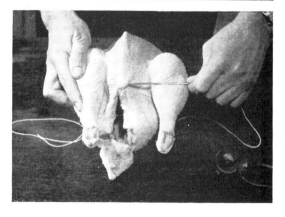

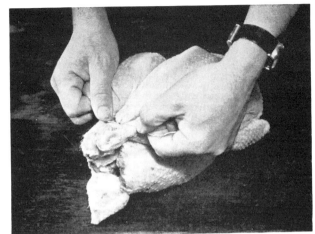

Take each string in turn and loop it over the knuckle of the joint. Draw the strings tightly together across the knuckle and knot. Centre picture shows the finished bird trussed in the way suggested.

Local Trade

Without doubt, it pays to build up a local retail trade when table birds are produced on a modest scale. Apart from the Christmas trade, satisfied customers will often place a regular order throughout the year and this is a great help in planning production. The extra labour involved in plucking and dressing must, of course, be reflected in the price charged.

Display Dressing and Packing

When birds are sent away in market packs (*below*) they must be allowed to cool first and should then be packed in greaseproof paper and straw, taking care to put chickens of the same size in a given pack.

For direct retail sales you should consider packing each bird in a plastic bag, perhaps with your own printed brand name. If you are selling elsewhere—possibly to a local hotel—find out exactly how the birds should be presented when fixing the contract.

BROODIES MUST BE BROKEN

Prompt Action

Broodiness is a perfectly natural occurrence but is also one that calls for prompt action. It is confined almost exclusively to the heavy breeds and crosses and may become a serious nuisance during the warmer months.

A broody bird is easily detected. She sits on the nest all day, spreads herself well out and, if disturbed, utters a distinctive squawk, stiffens her body and raises her feathers.

Slatted Floor Coop

If left many days a broody will cease laying and may not start again for a considerable time. To be effective, therefore, "treatment" must begin as soon as she is spotted. Put broody hens in a slatted floor coop, in sight of other birds, where the somewhat uncomfortable conditions and flow of air beneath, will usually break the habit.

Bottom photo gives an underneath view of a broody coop.

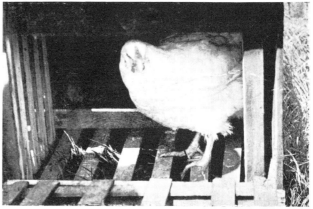

Siting the Coop

The wall of an intensive house may be used as the back of the coop, which should be raised from the ground. Give the birds protection, when necessary, from very hot sun or driving rain. Another way of checking broodiness is to run the offending bird, or birds, with a cockerel. If this happens to be convenient it is probably the quickest method of all, providing there are no nest boxes to which the hens can retreat.

Maintain Normal Diet

A mistaken idea is that of keeping food and water from the birds whilst they are broody. This is a great mistake for it will do little to break broodiness. On the other hand, it will almost certainly cause a loss of condition which may lead to a breakdown in egg production.

The normal diet should be continued, therefore, and fresh water should be available at all times. A little greenfood or grass meal will also be appreciated, especially if the birds have had access to grass previously.

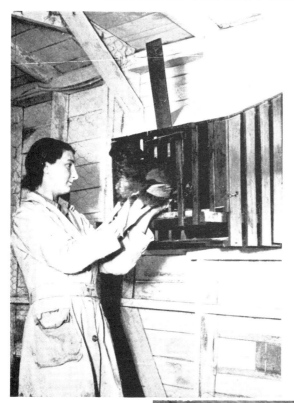

Wall Coop

In intensive houses the broody coops are often hung on the walls. They should be placed away from draughts but in a spot where there is plenty of light and in full view of the other birds.

Pullets or hens which have shown a marked tendency to broodiness should not be retained for breeding, unless excelling in some other respect, as the trouble is heritable. It is a simple matter to put leg rings on birds which have to be cooped. If this policy is followed rigorously for a number of seasons the factor will largely disappear.

Spare Cages

Spare battery cages (*right*) make excellent broody coops if nothing else is available. Birds kept in batteries in the normal way seldom go broody.

The domestic poultry-keeper who has not got a coop can often cure broodiness by letting the bird loose in the garden or on a spare piece of ground. If broodiness is not advanced, the interest provided by the change in surroundings will usually be enough to check the desire to sit.

THE MOULT

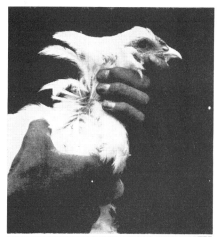

Birds with a high rate of production are generally the last to shed their feathers and are also the quickest in growing new ones. Poor producers may hang in the moult from early summer to late autumn, dropping only an occasional feather.

Bird in the top photo has a neck moult, a condition which may occur at any time of the year but is generally brought on by some error in feeding or management. Production may not cease for long but it often occurs in the high-price period. The other birds (*centre and bottom left*) are in varying stages of the moult, which generally starts on the back of the neck, works round to the front, and then spreads to breast and body. Feeding during the moult should be as for birds in full production.

The rate of moulting can also be detected by examination of the wing (*below*). This fairly rapid moulter has dropped a number of primaries within a short time of each other, making the wing look ragged. In a slow moulter the new feathers would be almost fully grown before the outer primaries dropped.

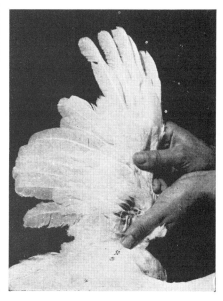

Yearling birds are sometimes induced to moult earlier than they normally would so as to bring them back into production at a time when eggs are scarce. This is called force-moulting and usually takes place in early August.

The moult is induced by restricting the birds' food to bran, or bran and a little grain, until the feathers fall freely (*above*). From then on, full feeds of normal mash must be given (*below*) for condition will be lost if the restricted diet is continued.

THE MALE BIRD

Individual Feeding

BECAUSE male birds are aggressive and apparently well able to look after themselves there is sometimes a tendency to neglect them. Nothing could be more unwise. To keep in first-class condition they must be carefully fed, preferably individually, for they will often allow their hens to get the best of the food, and may then lose condition or even moult (*top left photo*). A special trough or box, just too high for the hens to reach, is the best plan.

Crowing

Crowing can be a nuisance in built-up areas but it is doubtful whether attempts to stop this are wise. Early morning crowing can be discouraged to some extent by fastening wire netting a little above the level of the perching birds' heads as cocks invariably stand and stretch their necks upwards to crow (*top right photo*).

Some six weeks before the breeding pens are formed the spurs of the older males should be removed to prevent them damaging the hens' backs. The tips are cut off with wire cutters or may be burned down with a poker. Only the tips need removing.

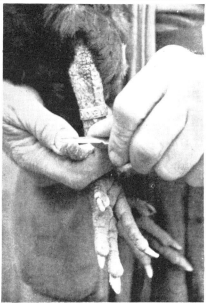

Removal of Spurs

Frost Bite Danger

The large combs carried by the male birds of some breeds are liable to frost bite in very severe weather. Apart from the pain this will cause, it will also have a serious effect on fertility. If you do not wish to resort to dubbing, apply Vaseline to the comb and wattles during frosty weather (*right*) and provide drinking vessels which do not cause these parts to get wet.

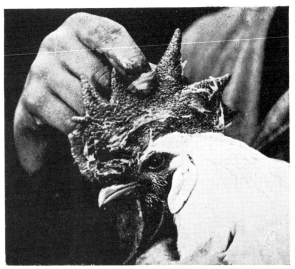

Dubbing

Ideally, dubbing should be performed when a cockerel is no more than three months old but the operation can be carried out on fully grown birds. Such pain as it causes is a good deal less than the prolonged suffering occasioned by frost bite.

The comb and wattles are best removed by using special dubbing scissors. This is a fairly simple operation, but get someone to show you before attempting it. Within a few days the male bird should be recovered.

Running cold water will check the considerable bleeding which occurs and Friar's Balsam applied afterwards is the best dressing. Isolate the bird in a warm coop for two or three days.

Should frost bite occur in undubbed birds, massaging between the palms of the hand may restore the circulation if started in time.

Massage for Frost Bite

FEATHER PICKING AND EGG EATING

OVERCROWDING and boredom are the most usual causes of feather picking, a vice which sometimes occurs with intensively-housed birds. Bare patches appear on various parts of the body. The habit may develop into cannibalism if not checked in time.

Treat Bare Patches

Bare patches should be dressed with Stockholm tar while a good deterrent, if the trouble is not too far advanced, is the water in which quassia chips have been soaked, this being applied to the feathers around the affected parts. Most important of all, provide greenfood and scratch feeds to keep the birds occupied.

Battery birds (*right*) frequently pull feathers from each other's necks.

That other vice, egg-eating, is also a trouble that is easier to prevent than to cure. Likewise, if it does occur it needs checking promptly.

Prevention lies in providing dark nest boxes and in ensuring that there is sufficient nesting space to prevent overcrowding. The latter state leads sooner or later to an egg getting broken and this is sufficient to give one or two birds a taste for the contents. From this they soon learn to break them for themselves. In a dark nest box (*top photo*) this seldom occurs, and sacks may be hung over the fronts of open-fronted nests for the same purpose.

Another good idea is to provide the sort of false floor seen in the picture, the egg passing through the hole in the netting to soft straw beneath. If the culprits can be caught at the start of the trouble they are best killed and sold.

Dark Nest Box

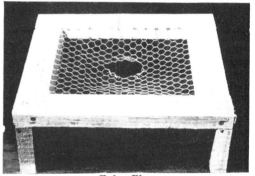

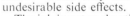

False Floor

Debeaking

Debeaking is an unfortunate necessity when outbreaks of feather picking and cannibalism are likely to assume serious proportions. It is not so much that the operation causes the birds any great discomfort but simply that the act of catching and handling them is just another "stress factor" which may have undesirable side effects.

The job is not so drastic as it sounds. Only the tip of the upper beak need be removed in most cases, though up to a third may be necessary in more serious outbreaks. The job can be done with sharp clippers or, better, with an electric debeaker which also cauterises the cut. Experience will tell you whether to debeak as a routine operation or only when an outbreak of vice occurs.

AILMENTS AND DISEASE

Light Sussex Bantam Cockerel

(Courtesy: Hall & Sons)

Watch for Healthy Birds

Although obvious it is not always appreciated that the best way to avoid disease is to keep birds which are naturally healthy.

When purchasing stock look for birds with the following:

    (a) glossy plumage
    (b) bright red comb
    (c) clear, bright eye
    (d) birds which are alert
           and active.

Avoid birds with shrunken faces, shrivelled combs, dishevelled plumage and any other signs of weakness. They will not lay many eggs and obviously cannot be relied upon to breed. The illustrations show healthy specimens.

Black Rosecomb Bantam Cockerel

(Courtesy: B.M. Dent)

Disease and the Environment

There is a definite relationship between the environment in which birds are reared and managed and the danger of disease. Free range birds (above) tend to be relatively free of disease yet can suffer from specific diseases more than birds reared intensively. For example, chicks reared on grass will be healthy but they are apt to contract coccidiosis which can be picked up from the ground. On the other hand, they do not suffer much from respiratory diseases, such as infectious brochchitis, which are a major problem with birds kept intensively on deep litter (below). This shows two Cobb broilers at the age of 49 days.

(*Courtesy*: Cobb Breeding Co. Ltd.)

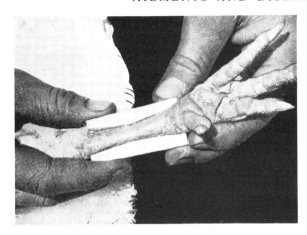

Broken Leg

Though not a frequent occurrence, accidents of this kind are well worth treating for they do not normally show any constitutional weakness like so many of the other minor ailments. Indeed, few poultry farmers bother to doctor sick birds because they are a danger to the health of the flock. But even one bird represents a high percentage of a back-garden pen and here treatment is often justified.

Use Splints

Splints are used to hold a broken leg, a pair being cut out of wood to fit the shank. While held firmly in position they are bound round with adhesive tape (*left*) and the job finished off without any loose ends (*below*). Keep the bird by herself in a warm coop until the leg has healed.

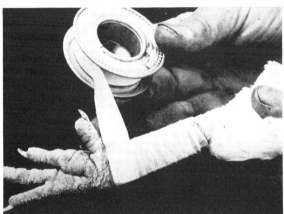

Hygienic Poultry Keeping

Disease in the flock is far less likely to occur when the housing and premises are kept clean and standard hygienic practices observed. Clean the troughs and water vessels regularly and ensure that the water is always clean. Clean droppings boards twice weekly. Thoroughly clean and disinfect all houses and equipment between successive batches of poultry: leave houses empty for three weeks after disinfection. Isolate newly-purchased stock for three weeks and during this time satisfy yourself that they are free from disease. Similarly, clean second hand equipment scrupulously before use. Finally, seek veterinary advice if you are in doubt.

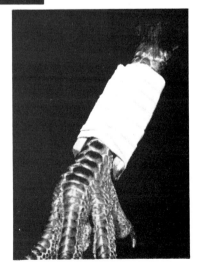

Colds

Colds are just one form of the many and complicated respiratory troubles which may affect poultry. This range of infections is often classified under the general heading of Chronic Respiratory Disease (C.R.D.) Though a number of different agents—bacterial, virus and fungus—are responsible, it has been proved that housing and management play a major part in "triggering-off" outbreaks. Inadequate ventilation is a major cause but any undue "stress factor"—poor feeding, sudden changes in rations or management, chilling, etc.— may lead to outbreaks.

C.R.D. Sufferer

The bird in the picture is a typical sufferer. Symptoms include general listlessness and a discharge from the eyes and nose, sometimes accompanied by difficulty in breathing. Control lies largely in improved hygiene and management and the prevention of stress, but treatment with antibiotics may prove effective. In the case of small back-garden flocks it may be worth treating an individual case by dipping the bird's beak in a solution of permanganate of potash every few hours (below), using the fingers to clear as much mucus as possible. Appetites may be encouraged by feeding a wet mash.

Fowl Pest

Though often taken to refer only to Newcastle disease, the term fowl pest applies equally to fowl plague. Suspected outbreaks of either must be notified to the police.

Symptoms of Newcastle disease may include a sudden drop in production, combined with listlessness and loss of appetite. Greenish yellow diarrhœa is often present, also rapid, noisy breathing, head twitching and partial paralysis. There may be a discharge from the eyes and nostrils. Death rate is variable.

Some of these symptoms might also occur with a fowl plague outbreak but there would certainly be high and sudden mortality. In either case, report your suspicions immediately.

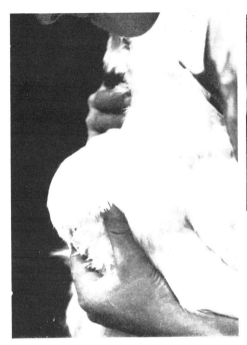

Crop Binding

Crop Troubles

Crop binding is usually caused by the bird eating stalky hay, straw or long grass, this getting lodged in the crop and collecting a mass of other food around it. If many birds do this there is likely to be some reason for their depraved appetite and this should be sought at once. A common fault is that of putting birds out on to long grass when they have been kept intensively. The grass should be kept short at least until the first craving for fresh greenfood has worn off.

Sour crop may also be caused by a blockage in the crop, a small obstruction causing other food to accumulate and become sour. It appears also that some constitutional weakness will give rise to the trouble, for "cured" cases very frequently succumb again.

A typical case of crop trouble is seen at top right. The swelling is obvious and the bird is clearly miserable. If the swelling is hard (*top left*) suspect crop binding: if soft (*lower photo*) sour crop is the trouble. In the latter case the contents may be massaged out if the bird is held upside down, afterwards giving the bird a small dose of bicarbonate of soda or Milk of Magnesia. If the trouble re-occurs kill the bird.

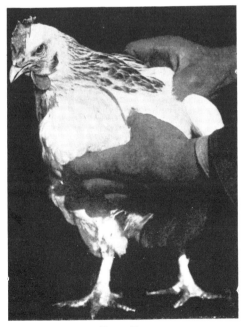

Sour Crop

Wash your hands before starting the operation—first with soap and water and then in a mild disinfectant solution. The knife, needle and thread to be used should first be boiled and the skin wiped with a disinfectant solution before the incision is made. Later, dress the stitched cut with an antiseptic ointment.

How to Operate for Crop Binding

There is only one thing to be done in severe cases of crop binding (when the contents are hard and large) and that is to operate. It is not a difficult task but an assistant is required to hold the bird still. The feathers are plucked from a small area over the centre of the crop (*above*) and a cut just over an inch long is made through the outer skin and the wall of the crop (*below left*). Either a razor blade or a very sharp knife should be used for this.

Use a spoon, button hook, or piece of stiff, bent wire to remove the contents of the crop, taking the greatest care not to tear the cut further. Wash the crop out with boiled water (allowed to cool, of course) and then sew up the cuts in the crop and outer skin separately, making about three stitches in each wound. Confine the bird to a warm coop for several days, starving her the first day and then feeding on soft, nourishing foods until she recovers.

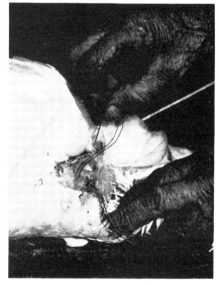

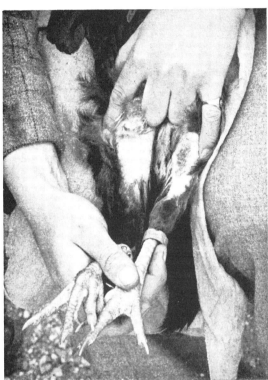

Fowl Pox

The early symptoms of birds affected with fowl pox are almost indistinguishable from those with colds or roup. But there soon appear small growths, not unlike warts, on the head, comb and wattles.

In case of doubt summon a vet, isolating all affected stock. Once it gets a hold, the disease spreads rapidly and mortality may be high. If your suspicions are confirmed, it is wisest to kill the birds affected and afterwards disinfect the premises.

Fowl pox can be prevented by vaccination but it takes two weeks for immunity to develop. Feathers are plucked from a patch on one leg and the area scratched with a scarifier until red (*lower photo*) and the vaccine painted on. A successful take is seen on the right in the upper photo.

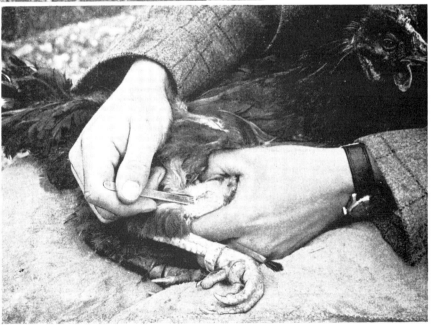

Fowl Paralysis

Fowl paralysis is the most easily recognised form of the disease known as lymphomatosis. Some typical victims are seen on this page. Symptoms will vary, depending on which of the nerves are affected, but it is usual for a leg or a wing to be paralysed first. The disease may possibly be transmitted in the egg, and can certainly be contracted in the first few weeks of life, but it is not generally seen until the pullet comes into lay.

Other forms of this disease include the common visceral type,

in which tumours form on the internal organs, and the ocular type. Another disease, leucosis is very hard to distinguish from the visceral form of lymphomatosis. As no complete cure is known, preventive methods must aim principally at the building up of strains resistant to the disease. Young chicks should not be allowed possible contact with the disease.

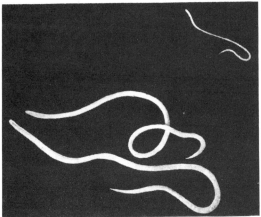

The Large Round Worm

Internal Parasites

Though worms seldom cause death they can result in much unthriftiness. They are commonly found where poultry are run on the same land for many years in succession, or in over-stocked yards. Control lies in breaking the worms' life cycle (they do not breed inside the birds) by resting or cropping the land regularly and by keeping the birds under clean conditions.

Found in the small intestine (*above*) it may be up to 3 in. or 4 in. long. The eggs, laid by the female worm whilst it is in the fowl, pass out in the droppings and can remain alive for several months until they are picked up by another bird. Once eaten, a worm emerges from the egg and the whole process begins again.

The caecal worm (*right*) is much smaller, being a bare ½ in. long. Its life cycle is similar to that of the round worm. Caecal worms do no great harm unless present in abnormally large numbers, for it has been shown that the majority of this country's flocks are infected.

Caecal Worm

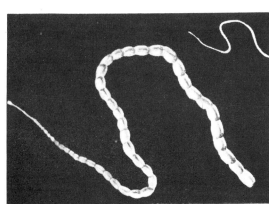

Tape Worm

There are several sorts of tape worm but they all differ from the varieties mentioned above in that the eggs must pass through an intermediate host—a fly, earthworm, slug, etc.—to complete their life cycle. Elimination of these hosts affords the best means of control, though modern drugs are quite effective. Tape worms vary greatly in size but are distinguishable by their segmented appearance.

Worm Symptoms

The common symptoms of a heavy worm infestation are diarrhœa, listlessness and a general loss of appetite and condition. The specimen on the right is obviously heavily infested, while the squat attitude of the fowl in the centre photo is also typical of the loss of vitality brought about by worms.

The miserable specimen below is the sort of bird most likely to fall prey to worms. Healthy, vigorous birds have greater powers of resistance though they, too, will succumb if kept under bad conditions. For accurate diagnosis the birds' droppings should be examined for whole or part worms.

Treatment

For large round worms, use one of the piperazine compounds. These are available,

with instructions, from veterinary chemists.

Phenothiazine is the most effective drug for expelling caecal worms, though in most cases it may not be worth while going to this trouble. This, too, is available from veterinary chemists.

Phenothiazine is also useful for getting rid of tape worms but butynorate is probably the best drug for this purpose.

Egg Binding

It sometimes happens that a bird is unable to pass a particularly large egg without assistance. This trouble is known as egg binding. Inability to lay may also be caused by muscular weakness or an obstruction but these causes are comparatively rare. The symptoms are very easily recognized. The affected bird will be seen on the nest for long periods, trying to pass the egg and soon becomes miserable and dejected (*above*).

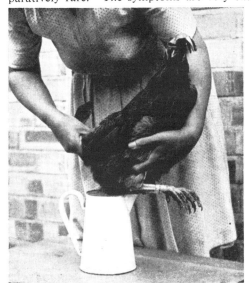

Steaming the Vent

Treatment

Treatment is quite simple but its success will depend on the size of the egg and on whether the bird has become very exhausted. Fill a jug with boiling water and hold the bird with her vent an inch or so above the top for five minutes. Then very gently lubricate the vent with Vaseline up to the point where the egg can be felt and put the bird back in the nest box. If she is still unable to lay, the egg must be broken with a probe, taking the greatest care not to scratch the egg passage and to remove every particle of egg. Keep the bird isolated for a few days.

Prolapsus

Pullets in full production are most liable to this trouble. The bird should be isolated, and the protruding parts replaced after being washed with tepid, boiled water. If repeated treatment has no effect, kill her.

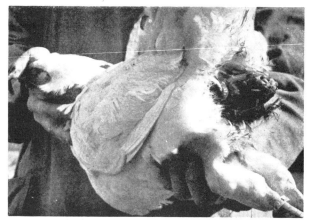

Dosing a Fowl

The bird should be held firmly on the lap with the left arm and the head held as in the photograph. Slight pressure with the thumb and forefinger will open the mouth.

Crooked Toes

This trouble, seen in chicks up to eight weeks of age, is more prevalent in some strains and may also be connected with the use of infra-red lamps. Slight and moderate cases are seen below. There is no cure and affected birds are best used for table when sufficiently grown.

A Case of Rickets

Chick Troubles

A typical case of rickets is seen above. This disease is caused by a deficiency of vitamin D and/or minerals. The trouble can be prevented (and cured if detected in the early stages) by the addition of 1 per cent cod liver oil to the mash, and the provision of a balanced mineral mixture.

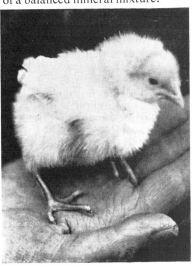

B.W.D.

Chicks may die from this disease from the fourth day onwards without showing any signs of ill health but often they appear sleepy and dishevelled (*left*). Furazolidone is the most effective drug for treatment. (*See pages* 131, 132.)

Coccidiosis

There are two forms of this disease which may affect chickens. Caccal

(*Continued on next page*)

(Coccidiosis continued)

coccidiosis causes heavy losses during the first two months of life: intestinal coccidiosis attacks growers and even adult birds. A typical case of the former is seen in the centre photo on previous page: note the drooping wings, ruffled feathers and general wretchedness.

Prevention and Cure

However, such symptoms are not always evident and a few chicks may die without showing any signs of distress. The cycle of infection can be broken by moving the chicks to clean land every other day or by renewing the litter at similar intervals. The disease is most prevalent under damp, warm conditions. Several drugs give effective control: some, such as nitrofurazone, are used for continuous feeding at preventive level; others, notably the sulpha drugs, are given at a higher concentration when an outbreak occurs.

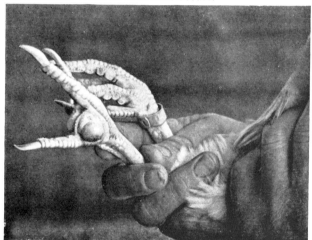

Intestinal Coccidiosis

The build-up of this form is generally slow, though it does sometimes show itself suddenly.

Actual losses are not so severe as with the caecal type but many birds become unthrifty, losing weight and appetite steadily. Prevention and cure of the disease is the same as for caecal coccidiosis.

Bumble Foot

A cut or blister on a bird's foot sometimes becomes septic, leading to a distinct swelling (*above*). This condition, known as bumble foot, is seldom noticed until the bird is actually lame or clearly reluctant to put one foot on the ground. The swelling should be lanced, emptied, packed with penicillin cream or sulphonamide powder and bandaged.

PARASITES WHICH LOWER VITALITY

Red Mite

OF the many parasites which may infect poultry the red mite is the most troublesome. These tiny pests live by sucking the birds' blood, thereby lowering vitality to such an extent that death may occur in some extreme cases. They do this at night, spending the day on the walls of the house, in crevices, nest boxes and where they can escape the daylight.

It stands to reason that a light, airy house is much less likely to be infested, while all fittings should be removable so as to assist cleaning.

Infestation in Perch Socket

Even if the mites are not suspected it is wise to make a regular inspection of crevices near the perches so that an outbreak may be checked before it gets a hold. A typical infestation in a perch socket is seen in the top picture. Below this is a useful metal socket, less likely to harbour the mites.

Metal Socket

Method of Destruction

To destroy red mites, clean the house and all the fittings thoroughly with a brush and hot water and then paint or spray with a paraffin-creosote mixture (equal parts). Paint the underside of the perches with a similar mixture or 40 per cent nicotine sulphate at weekly intervals.

There are also aerosol dispensers sold for treating whole houses or small areas (left). Red mite can live in an empty house for up to six months.

Anti-pest Aerosol

Depluming Mite

It is not always easy to distinguish feather plucking from the effects of the tiny depluming mite (*top photo*). Itself responsible for bare patches on the bird's body, it also sets up an intense irritation which is a frequent cause of feather plucking outbreaks. The mite does not appear usually until the warm spring weather. Treat the affected parts with oil of carroway ointment, having first isolated the affected birds to prevent the mites spreading.

Lice

A heavy infestation of lice may also lead to loss of feathers (*below*). The parasites are grey in colour and are easily detected moving over the skin when the feathers are parted. A thorough dusting with Gammexane or D D T powder is the easiest control measure.

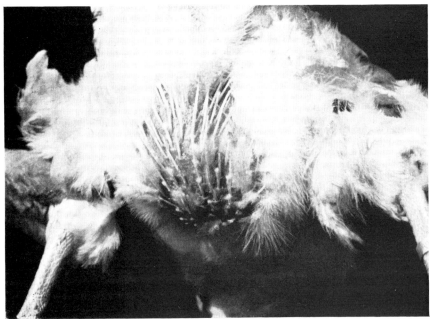

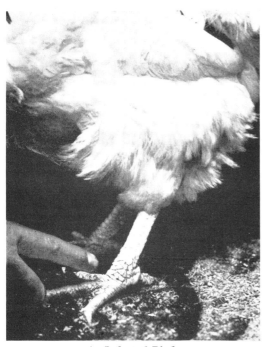

An Infected Bird

Simple Treatment

Scaly Leg

Presence of the scaly leg mite is often, though not always, associated with rather dirty conditions. Older birds are always more susceptible to attack.

In neglected cases the trouble may cause lameness and the affected fowl will be seen standing or squatting for long periods, reluctant to move. But long before this stage is reached the effects of the mites' presence can be seen on the bird's feet and legs (*top photo*) where the scales will be raised giving a coarse, rough appearance.

Treatment

There are a number of effective treatments, the mite being among the easiest of poultry parasites to kill. Simplest is that of dipping the leg in a small jar of paraffin, gently scrubbing it with a small brush when removed. The photo shows how the jar can be held firmly and this is a safer method than the commonly used bucket, for the paraffin must not be allowed to touch the flesh above the hock.

Another treatment is to brush the scales with warm, soapy water and then dress with a sulphur ointment.

Difficult to Detect

As it causes little discomfort in the early stages, and does not affect appetite or vitality, scaly leg is the sort of trouble most often detected by the poultry-keeper who examines and handles his poultry at frequent intervals. It will go unnoticed by the man who waits for a bird to show unmistakable signs of illness before taking action.

Dusting Safeguards

The list of lice, fleas, bugs and mites which may live on poultry is somewhat formidable. Clean, light airy conditions are not conducive to heavy infestations of external parasites, however, while regular dusting is a further safeguard during the spring and summer months.

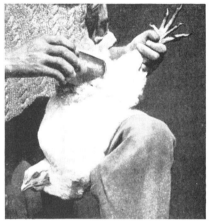

Special powders may be purchased for dusting poultry or a general purpose D D T or Gammexane powder used. Photos on this page show how the fowl should be held for dusting various parts of the body, the places of greatest importance being under the wings and under the tail (*shown above and right*).

Dust Broody Hens

Before setting a broody hen she should be thoroughly dusted all over, taking care not to get the powder in her eyes. The dark and warmth of the coop is an ideal place for the rapid increase of parasites. A sprinkler is needed for dispensing the powder. A small pepper pot is useful. Make sure the powder goes beneath the feathers and on to the skin, for the bird will shake off the surplus on being released.

Outdoor Dust Bath

The hen's natural method of cleaning herself is in the dust bath. Without doubt, too, the birds get considerable pleasure from the process. On range they will make their own baths but if an outdoor dust bath is provided in a semi-intensive unit it may prevent unsightly scoops being made in the grass. A low covering will keep the contents in the necessary dry state.

Use for Garden Frame

A large box, or the sides of a garden frame, make a useful container for a dust bath in a covered run or intensive house. Soil, sand and a few ashes are the best contents, these being lightly dusted with an insect powder every week. Renew at frequent intervals.

Daily Dust Bath

Always ensure that broody hens (*below*) have some spot for a daily dust bath. This is necessary both before and after hatching.

Spray with Creosote

The interiors of semi-intensive houses should be sprayed or painted with creosote each year as a routine measure against insect parasites and disease. The walls and ceilings of intensive houses are better lime-washed after disinfection. Hand pumps and stirrup pumps are quite effective.

Pay special attention to the under-side of perches. Have them outside in the daylight and see that the liquid enters all the crevices. Battery plants must receive a thorough cleaning and disinfection annually. A 4 per cent soda solution is quite good. Most effective, but more expensive, is the portable steam sterilizer seen below.

Cleaning a Battery Plant

FOXES AND OTHER VERMIN

Folds Best Solution

POULTRY farmers who have suffered know only too well the damage a single fox can do overnight (*centre photo*). Unless the netting is high and kept in perfect condition, even semi-intensive units are not safe in infested areas. Where the whole flock is not housed intensively, folds are the best solution for they are quite fox-proof if kept in good condition (*above*).

Watch Dog

It is sometimes said that a coating of tar or creosote on the netting will keep foxes away from poultry runs. The idea is worth trying, anyway. A more certain safeguard is a fox hound or other reliable watch dog. Badgers are known to take poultry on occasion, too, but these animals are not nearly so troublesome as foxes.

Jackdaws and crows soon learn to raid the feed troughs of birds fed out of doors, while the crows are not averse to picking up a stray chick. If the trouble gets out of hand a funnel trap will catch them in large numbers when baited with mash or corn, especially if a live bird can be put inside as a decoy.

Funnel Trap

Rats and Mice

Few poultry farms are entirely without rats. Many are heavily infested. Yet these rodents, and to a lesser extent mice, are responsible for an appalling annual loss to the industry. Almost any food eaten by poultry is attractive to them and young chicks are easy prey unless kept in a rat-proof house or coop. Finally, they are notorious as spreaders of disease and vermin.

Routine Safeguards

Concrete, corrugated iron and small mesh netting are the materials with which to rat-proof a house. Wood-floored houses must be raised well above the ground. Outdoor feed hoppers should have guards on the legs to prevent the rats climbing and wet mash troughs must be left quite empty at night. Feed sliced roots in the troughs, never on the ground. Corn, meal, waste bread, etc., should be stored in bins, never on shelves or on the floot (*top and bottom photos*).

Poison

Traps and poison may be used for eliminating rats. Warfarin based poisons are very effective and should be placed where birds or other animals cannot reach them.

DUCKS

BECAUSE of low packing-station prices for their eggs, ducks are seldom kept for large-scale production. But flocks of a dozen or so are much more popular and have much to commend them. They are capable of quite astonishing laying performances, 250 eggs per bird annually being an average yield. Housing is much less costly than for pullets and disease problems are few.

In contrast, table duck production is mostly in the hands of large producers. Even so, there is reasonable scope here for the smaller poultry farmer who takes the precaution of finding a reliable market before commencing production.

BREEDS FOR EGGS AND TABLE

The Khaki Campbell

THE Khaki Campbell is undoubtedly the best breed for egg production. It also gives a fair table carcase, though in this direction it is not to be compared with the Aylesbury. Because of its value as an egg producer (yields of over 300 eggs are quite common in laying tests) it is more widely kept than the other breeds, and it is only natural that there should be a substantial difference in the output of the different strains. Pay great attention to this point when buying Khaki ducklings.

Breed Points

Adult Khaki Campbells weigh between 4 lb. and 5 lb., the drakes weighing about $\frac{1}{2}$ lb. more than the ducks. The drakes are fine-looking birds (*above*) with

their bronze and khaki feathering, dark orange legs and feet and green bill. The ducks (*right*) are khaki all over.

The white eggs of the Khaki Campbell weigh $2\frac{1}{2}$ oz. or more. Many people consider that a duck egg, besides being larger than a chicken's, has more flavour. Good strains lay throughout the year and do not require such elaborate housing as chickens. On the other hand, food consumption is greater though ducks are excellent foragers when allowed range.

Khaki Campbell Duck

White Campbell

The White Campbell

The White Campbell is similar to the Khaki in conformation, having been developed from the white sports which that breed sometimes throws. It is not such a good layer as the Khaki but it has proved valuable for crossing with Aylesburys. The breed is seldom seen nowadays.

Before the Khaki Campbell became established, the Indian Runner was easily the best duck for egg production. A great many strains still excel in this respect but the breed has lost commercial popularity on account of its poor table qualities. They are also temperamental birds, easily upset by moves and disturbances and do not do well under restricted condition. Runners lay medium size eggs.

There are five varieties of Runners but they differ only in colouring. All have the same unique upright stance and fine, graceful appearance. Most popular are White Runners (*right*), Fawn, and Fawn and White. A mixed pen of Fawn, and Fawn and White Runners is seen below. Average weights are about 4 lb. for ducks and 4½ lb. for drakes.

White Runner

A Mixed Pen of Runners

Aylesbury

Muscovy Ducks

Muscovies are not of great commercial value but are still kept on many general farms (often finding much of their own living) because of their large size and consequent table value in the farmhouse. There are several variations in colouring. Laying is confined mainly to the warmer months.

The Aylesbury (*left*) is the supreme table duck. It grows quickly and weighs between 9 lb. and 10 lb. when mature. Pure Aylesburys have the pinkish-white skin which is required of a first-class table bird. The bill is pink, the legs and feet bright orange and the plumage a uniform white. Aylesburys are poor layers, though the eggs are large. From February to June is the normal laying season.

Though a better layer than the Aylesbury, the Pekin has yellowish flesh, a definite disadvantage in table birds. However, the progeny of an Aylesbury-Pekin cross are mostly white-skinned and this mating is widely adopted. Adult drakes weigh about 8½ lb. and adult ducks 7½ lb. Both sexes have creamy plumage and yellow bills.

Pekin

HOUSING

Ducks can live throughout the year without any sort of housing or cover but they will not lay well. Some sort of protection is needed at night if production is to be maintained in cold weather and this will also encourage the table breeds to lay earlier in the year.

Three simple types of housing are shown on this page. In the top one, hurdles are employed to keep the ducks confined until after the morning feed, by which time nearly all the eggs will have been laid. In the centre is a small home-made house for half a dozen ducks while an ordinary semi-intensive poultry house is being used in the lower photo.

Slatted floors should be fitted when possible and 3–4 sq. ft. of floor space allowed for each

Hurdle Fencing

Simple Home-made House

duck. If the entrance is above ground level, fix a sloping board as leg injuries may result if the ducks have to fly or jump in and out. A fairly wide entrance is best.

Site the house on well-drained ground and, if possible, move it at frequent intervals. Ducks will soon turn heavy, wet land into a quagmire. So long as there is sufficient ventilation, without draughts, the darker the inside of the house the better.

Semi-Intensive Poultry House

Simple Duck House

Simple but effective is the type of duck house shown on this page. The wire netting front is hinged so that it also serves as a ramp. The generous eave keeps out driving rain and also bright moonlight—a frequent cause of disturbance.

Whether or not a slatted floor is fitted, a generous depth of straw bedding should be provided. This will need renewing once a week. Earth floors are not suitable, as the house soon becomes rat-infested, but rammed chalk is satisfactory.

Renewal of Straw Bedding

Permanent Runs

Light, well-drained land is needed when ducklings are reared in permanent runs, as above. It is important to provide alternate runs for each pen. The system is not much used for adult ducks as each bird must be allowed up to 25 sq. yds. of run area if the grass is not to suffer.

Less costly and more hygienic are sun parlours fitted with slatted floors. Under this system the growing ducklings get the sun and air which they undoubtedly need but are kept dry underfoot and take up little space. The system is widely used for rearing table ducklings.

Sun Parlour with Slatted Floor

Housing Table Ducks

Straw housing and lightly-strawed runs are suitable for rearing relatively small batches of table ducklings. The runs should be on a slope, with the water supply at the lower end of the slope. Small brooder houses, with wire-floored verandas (*left*) make good first-stage quarters for table ducklings. Drinking water is given outside after the first day or so. The ducklings feather and harden-off rapidly under such conditions.

Some table duck producers are now housing their birds intensively on wire throughout (*below*) with access to a veranda during the second part of the fattening period.

FEEDING

Eᴍᴘᴛʏ troughs (*above*) after about 20 minutes feeding show that the right amount of food has been given. Ample trough space (*left*) helps to prevent jostling or fighting. It is a good idea to tip the grain feed into a trough full of water (*below*) to give the ducks occupation.

The quantity of grain and mash eaten by a laying duck depends on whether it has free range or only a very restricted run. In the latter case up to $\frac{1}{2}$ lb. of food will be needed daily, but $\frac{1}{4}$ lb. may be sufficient for birds on range. *Ad lib* feeding of pellets is successful for birds in small runs but a less wasteful system is to give morning and evening wet mash feeds, with grain at mid-day.

Popular Foods

Wheatings, maize meal, ground oats, bran and fish meal are amongst the foods commonly given to ducks. A suitable meal ration for laying ducks is wheatings, 4 parts; bran, 2 parts; maize meal,

(*Continued on next page*)

A wire netting platform around the drinking bowl will prevent the surrounding ground becoming a quagmire. Such a container needs emptying at least twice daily, so it is important to have a water supply close at hand and to have some means of disposing of the dirty water. Failing this, the conditions seen in the lower photo may soon occur.

Wire Netting Platform

(Feeding continued)

2 parts; ground oats, 2 parts; fish meal $1\frac{1}{4}$ parts. Add 1 per cent cod liver oil during the winter months. Laying ducks should have access to flint and limestone grit at all times.

Maize, wheat and clipped oats are the best grains for ducks. Between 1 oz. and 2 oz. per bird is the daily allowance. More than this may do harm by restricting the amount of mash, and therefore protein, eaten.

A popular fattening mash is wheatings, 4 parts; barley meal, 3 parts; fish meal, 1 part. However, as with laying ducks, it is now more usual to use one of the proprietary mashes compounded for stock of that particular type. Though costing more, one is assured of a properly-balanced feed providing a reputable brand is purchased.

Finally, make full use of cheap, or home-grown, potatoes, but in so doing make sure that the protein balance of the mash is not upset.

Poor Watering Arrangements

SOME GENERAL POINTS

Ponds—Natural and Artificial

WATER for swimming is not at all essential for ducks. What is most needed is a water container sufficiently deep for them to dip their beaks and eyes beneath the surface. But anyone who has kept ducks in natural surroundings knows how much they enjoy a swim. It is well worth while to make a simple artificial pond unless a natural pond or stream is available (*below*). Completely stagnant water should be avoided as it is liable to become a source of infection.

A cement pond is easily made, using a mixture of 1 part cement, $2\frac{1}{2}$ parts damp sand and 4 parts coarse aggregate. If possible, this should be put to set in a wooden mould but a reasonably good job can be done by laying the cement directly on to rammed earth. Build the pond close to a supply of water and provide it with a drainage pipe and stopper. Raise the sides slightly above the level of the surrounding ground and see that the surface of the cement is quite smooth. Loose stones make a good surround for such a pond.

Swimming in Natural Surroundings

Ducks or Fowls?

Ducks offer many advantages over fowls, but there are also a few snags. On the credit side, they are capable of laying more and bigger eggs than hens and they require little in the way of housing. Even more important, they are much hardier and are less prone to disease. Finally, ducklings grow a good deal quicker than cockerels.

Against this, they require more land, doing best on generous grass range (*top and bottom photos*). They are also more nervous than chickens and require gentle management. Uneasy birds (*right*) seldom lay well. Lastly, duck eggs generally fetch a lower price than hen eggs.

Quickly Panic

This picture shows clearly the sort of panic to which ducks are prone if frightened. An isolated instance may do little harm but constant disturbances will have a bad effect on egg production. Never allow ducks to be chased by a dog or to be worried by children. Once they have gained confidence they are friendly and intelligent creatures.

Handling and Management

Ducks should be handled as little as possible. They are nervous creatures and dislike disturbances. Similarly, the same attendant should feed them night and morning, collect their eggs, etc. and so gain their confidence.

When ducks have to be caught or handled for a particular purpose a folding hurdle (*below*) can be used to drive them quietly into a corner of the pen. If one side is kept a short distance from the wire each bird can be grasped, firmly but gently, by the neck, as it tries to escape. Talk to the birds throughout the operation and make no sudden movements.

Check to Laying

The practice of buying point-of-lay ducks is not always successful. The change of surroundings, food and attendant, as well as the journey may put the birds off lay for some time. If you are unable to rear your own ducklings, try to buy them at least a month or six weeks before they are due to lay.

Culling Guide

Some idea of a duck's value as a layer can be gained even before she is handled. The best birds are always on the move and are eager for their food. When on range, they are reluctant to return to the house at night. A duck in lay, or just about to lay, has a large abdomen, often nearly touching the ground (*right*). Poor ducks can be singled out by their thin, angular appearance, in contrast to the well-rounded lines of the rest of the flock.

Broodiness

Broodiness is not a serious problem but some birds will try to sit. Such ducks show much the same signs as broody hens, raising their feathers and making a distinctive noise when approached. If spotted in the early stages, broodiness is easily broken by confining the bird to a coop for a few days (*left*) away from the nest of her own choosing.

Is She in Lay ?

To hold a duck, rest the bird on the palm of one hand, its head facing your body, and place your other hand on its back. In this position it will remain quiet and calm. As with chickens, the distance between the pelvic bones gives an indication of whether or not the bird is in lay. If there is room for four fingers then she is certainly in lay: three fingers suggest that she is just beginning or ceasing production. There should also be room for four fingers between the pelvic and breast bones of a bird in lay

BREEDING

Selection and Mating

Trap nests are a great help in the selection of ducks for the breeding pen, but they should be introduced to them before they come into lay. The birds are put in them in the evening and are released at about 9 a.m. the next morning. A note is made of each egg laid, together with the duck's leg ring number.

Breeding Pens

With the egg-laying breeds such as Campbells and Runners, one drake should be allowed to six ducks. Only four ducks should be mated to each drake of the heavier table breeds. When flock mating is practised, a rather bigger ratio is possible. Three Campbell drakes should together manage up to 24 ducks.

Vigour and Good Health

As with all stock, vigour and good health are the key points when selecting stock for mating. Bright eyes, fine heads (*left*) and a lively alert appearance are good guides. Feathering should be tight and glossy. When handled, both ducks and drakes should have a good covering of flesh over their bones and be well up to standard weight for their breed.

Hatching and Rearing

A broody hen will cover about ten duck eggs: except that the eggs should be sprinkled with water daily during the later stages, management is the same as for hens' eggs. When an incubator is used, a dish of water should be placed in the centre of the egg tray, besides the normal moisture arrangement. Sprinkle the eggs twice daily during the last fortnight of the 28-day incubation period. With the bulb of the thermometer just clearing the eggs, maintain a temperature of 103°.

The Broody Hen

Ducklings are easily reared under a broody hen (*above*) or they may be reared with a standard type of brooder, or foster mother. Wire floors are useful for intensive rearing (*right*) but if at all possible a grass run should be provided (*below*). Temperature should be 85° for a start, being reduced by stages until the ducklings do without heat at four weeks.

Young Ducklings Coming Out of House

Four Weeks Old

Well-grown ducklings of four weeks old (*above*) can manage without artificial heat but the changeover should not be too rapid. As with chicks, a hurricane lantern or some other slight warmth should be given for the first few nights. Alternatively, their sleeping place should be well lined, and bedded with hay or soft straw so as to retain as much warmth as possible. Any check at this stage may have a serious effect on future growth so a little trouble is well repaid.

As already mentioned (p. 160), sun parlours or verandahs are excellent for rearing ducklings when space is limited. They can be used during the brooding stage if the floor is covered with small mesh netting and they are equally suitable when heat is dispensed with. A concrete base (*below*) is very much easier to keep clean than an earth floor and can be swilled with a hose as often as necessary. Part of the top of each verandah can be covered to provide shade during hot weather.

Sun Parlour with Concrete Base

Range Rearing

Ideally, ducklings should be reared on range. The exercise, grass and insect life are of the greatest value in promoting health and development. Only the simplest housing is needed but it should be sufficient to give shade during the day as well as a sleeping place for the night. Photos on this page show typical rearing arrangements; in both cases the houses and surrounds are easily moved to fresh ground as the grass gets eaten down and soiled. Table ducklings are mostly marketed when 8 to 10 weeks old. Khaki Campbells start to lay when four to five months old.

Methods of Sexing

Vent sexing of day-old ducklings is not particularly difficult but it requires some practice. Sexing by voice at about the eight-week stage is very much simpler: surplus drakes can then be sold off a little later. At this stage the females utter a distinct quack when grasped by the tail or wing, whereas the drakes can do no more than hiss. Later, the curved feathers above the drakes' tails are easily seen.

Eight Weeks Old

Up to eight weeks, young ducklings can be fed on standard baby chick mash. This should be given five or six times daily at first, the feeds being reduced gradually until three feeds are given when the ducklings are eight weeks old (*above*). At this age they can go on to a growers' mash. Instead of the wet mash, crumbs or pellets can be fed.

Ample, clean drinking water is an absolute necessity for ducklings (*below*). It should be deep enough for them to dip their head under but should have a guard to keep them from swimming in it and fouling it. Unless hatched under a duck, baby ducklings must on no account be allowed to swim as their feathers will at first lack the oil necessary to keep them afloat.

Clean Drinking Water

GEESE

GEESE come into their own where plenty of grazing is available. Under such conditions they can prove really profitable, as little supplementary feeding is needed for many months of the year. Yet geese for the Christmas market are often in short supply.

Grazing for geese must be of reasonably good quality. They are selective feeders and will ignore the coarser species of grass. But the boundary fences need be only two or three feet high and only the simplest housing is required.

POPULAR BREEDS

The Toulouse

THIS is the largest variety of domestic goose: adult weights of up to 30 lb. are not uncommon. Development is rather slow and the smaller breeds are more favoured nowadays for table purposes. The Toulouse lays well—sometimes as many as 50 eggs in a season—but is not a good sitter. Colour is steel grey and white.

The Buff Brecon

A small, compact variety. It is not very common outside Wales but is quite a useful table bird, the ganders weighing 17 lb. to 18 lb. and the geese a pound or so less. Colouring, as its name implies, is buff.

The Embden (*left*), like the Toulouse, is on the big side for today's needs. Crossed with a Roman gander, however, the quick-growing progeny weigh about 15 lb. at maturity as against the 18 lb. to 20 lb. of pure Embdens. Between 20 and 30 eggs are laid.

The Embden

Roman Geese

Roman geese (*above*) are possibly the best variety for running on the general farm. Adult birds seldom weigh more that 14 lb. These geese are excellent foragers, grow quickly and have plenty of meat in proportion to frame and offal. The females are good layers and will hatch and rear their own goslings, if desired.

Utility breeds of Chinese geese (*below*) have many of the qualities of the Roman and are even better layers. Yields of 100 eggs are not uncommon. There are two varieties—Fawn and White. Though the latter are less common, they are more suited to the table trade. Chinese geese are poor sitters.

Chinese Geese

Old English Crested

Old English Crested Geese are rarely seen nowadays. They are big birds and are mainly notable for the distinctive crest which is seen on the females' heads. Apart from the breeds mentioned in these pages, there are a number of ornamental varieties of geese, but these are not suitable for commercial production.

Mixed Breeding

The English breeds of geese are officially divided into three varieties—Grey, White and Grey-back. But inter-crossing has made it very difficult to decide the variety of many geese seen on the general farm (*above*). On the whole, they are small birds and extremely hardy. Egg production is generally poor. It is thought that these geese were originally bred from the wild Grey Lag goose.

HOUSING AND MANAGEMENT

GEESE are the hardiest of all domestic poultry and need no more than the simplest cover for protection at night. An open-fronted shed or straw bale house is quite sufficient though for permanent use a simple, covered pen, made of timber and corrugated iron or asbestos, looks neater and requires less maintenance.

Alternatively, an ordinary lean-to poultry house can be fitted with a sloping runway (*below*) and the windows removed and replaced with netting. On no account should geese be coddled as their natural hardiness and freedom from ailments are amongst their greatest assets. On sheltered farms they often sleep out all the year round.

Grazing Land

Geese are excellent grazers and on free range (up to a *maximum* of 20 geese to the acre) will find much of their own food for the greater part of the year.   Adult geese should have a mash feed in the morning, except when the grass is very lush and plentiful, and may also be given soaked grain in severe weather.

Grass Runs

Where poultry are kept on the semi-intensive system, geese can be of great value in keeping down grass in the runs during the flush season.   If they are moved as soon as they have cleared the grass, adult geese need little or no extra feeding.

Water Supply

Geese on range must have drinking water available at all times.   They should be able to dip their heads under the water but the container should not be so large that they try to swim in it. A stream is an advantage, of course, but not essential.

Finding the Eggs

Geese will not use the ordinary type of nest box but prefer to find some secluded spot of their own choosing. A few sheaves of straw placed in a corner of their shed (*left*) will very often attract them and the eggs should be removed from this daily.

Except on large farms, broody hens offer the easiest means of hatching. Though artificial hatching is often successful, the percentage of failures is much greater than with hen or duck eggs. If an incubator is used, the eggs should be sprayed lightly with warm water, twice daily, using a fine garden syringe. Run the machine at 102°.

A goose will cover up to 10 eggs, a hen up to 4. The incubation period is about 28 days.

Geese not Garden Birds

One frequently sees geese kept in small yards and gardens, but this is not to be recommended. They soon foul the ground and require a disproportionate amount of food when unable to graze. Grazing is, after all, one of their main assets and without it geese are not an economic proposition.

REARING

Rearing the Goslings

GOSLINGS are not at all difficult to rear, particularly as most hatchings take place in the late spring. When reared artificially, a hover placed in a field house (*above*) is the ideal arrangement. In mild weather the goslings will be out on the grass as soon as they have found their legs and can usually manage without heat when a week or ten days old.

When hatched under a hen (and remember to damp the eggs well during the last fortnight of incubation) or placed under a broody after artificial incubation, they are even less trouble and will often lose interest in their foster mother when under a fortnight old.

A hen will brood up to a dozen goslings but should be given a roomy coop as the goslings grow at a great rate. The coop should be placed on short grass and an area around it fenced with netting to prevent the young birds straying.

Rats are a danger to newly-hatched goslings. The coop or brooder house must give protection from these vermin at night. In chilly weather the brooder house should have a protected entrance to prevent draughts blowing under the hover.

Leg Weakness

Shade in Hot Weather

Freshly-hatched goslings are sometimes weak on their legs. An extreme case is seen on the right in the upper photo. The trouble is easily put right by tieing the legs loosely together to help them to stand and so gain strength.

Only the simplest housing is needed for growing goslings but shade must be provided in hot weather. In the centre photo the hinged side of a night ark serves the purpose Alternatively, a small thatched shelter could be built at little expense.

Five or six feeds of chick mash are needed each day during the first week. After this, four feeds are sufficient up to eight weeks and then only two need be given. Quantity is governed by the grazing available: each feed should be enough to keep them busy for ten minutes without leaving the trough for more than a moment or two. Feed the mash crumbly moist.

Clean water given in a flat dish should be freely available. Avoid upright or flimsy troughs for if the goslings *can* knock the container over they *will*.

Clean Water for Drinking

Specialist Plant

There are few specialist gosling producers but the photos show the interior of one such plant in Kent. Incubation and brooding takes place in the same building, all the young stock being sold at a week old. Over each protected brooding compartment an infra-red lamp is suspended. Warmth is controlled by raising or lowering the lamps until the goslings appear comfortable.

Infra-red Lamp for Rearing

Bright-emitter lamps are used. These are on day and night and it has been found that the goslings eat much more than when hen- or hover-reared. This has the effect of promoting growth and the week-old goslings are exceptionally large. Dry mash and water is provided *ad lib.*

Goslings on Range

Some breeds of geese, particularly Romans, sit well and are careful with the goslings which they hatch.   Others are unreliable sitters or are clumsy with their babies.   Geese sitting on their own eggs should be put in a roomy coop within sight of the other geese.   Moisten the eggs daily if the goose does not have a chance to swim when off the nest.

When hatched, the goose and goslings can run with the rest of the set (*above*) if the range is restricted.   Otherwise, it is better to keep them in a pen for the first week or so, moving this once or twice each day.

Goslings in Pen

TURKEYS

IN common with other branches of poultry farming, turkey production has undergone big changes in recent years. In this case the advances stem from efforts to popularise turkey as a year-round dish, instead of one reserved for Christmas, and also to rear birds competitive in price and quality with other classes of table poultry.

As yet, the revolution is by no means complete and there is considerable variation in quality of stock and management efficiency. It is suggested, though, that newcomers to turkey farming must be prepared to specialise if they are to keep abreast of increasing competition.

SOME POPULAR BREEDS

THE Norfolk Black (*left*) is a very popular medium-size breed which is extensively bred in the eastern counties. Flesh quality is excellent and there is also plenty of meat in proportion to bone. Egg production is relatively high and broodiness not a great problem. Feathering is black, shot with green. Weights range from 10 lb. to 15 lb., the stags weighing heaviest, of course.

Norfolk Black

The Broad-Breasted Bronze (*right and below*) is the largest turkey bred in the country. Stags frequently weigh from 25 lb. to 30 lb. and the female 15 lb. or more. Flesh quality is good and the proportion of meat on the breast is generally outstanding. Fewer eggs are laid than with Norfolk Blacks, though the eggs are somewhat larger. This breed is better suited to the catering trade than to domestic consumers.

Broad-Breasted Bronze

On the following pages will be seen a number of photos of white turkeys. These comprise two breeds, the Beltsville Small White (p. 188) and the British White (p. 189). Not shown is the up-and-coming Broad-Breasted White.

Stags of the former breed scale from 12 lb. to 16 lb., with 10 lb. being about the maximum for females. They mature early and lay well. British Whites are comparable in size to the Bronze. They carry plenty of breast meat and lay well.

Broad-Breasted Bronze

HOUSING AND RUNS

Many methods of housing and penning turkeys are adopted with success and choice of a system depends very much on the amount of land available and the scale of the undertaking. It is quite in order to house breeding birds intensively throughout the season. Each turkey requires about 10 sq. ft. of floor space. In this case, deep litter should be provided.

The type of shedding seen above is used on a great many small farms but the disadvantage here is that it cannot be moved to fresh ground. Range houses, mounted on wheels or skids, are more satisfactory. Alternatively, the birds can be driven daily from permanent houses on to pasture. Folds and straw yards also give good results.

A modern brooder house on an American experimental farm is seen below. Each run has a wire floor as a precaution against disease.

Pole Barns

Pole barns (*above*) are popular because they give a good degree of protection at low cost. Roofing on top of the pole supports consists of felt laid over a light timber and netting frame.

These Beltsville White breeding turkeys are running on a slatted-floor veranda. The slats are bottomed with wire and covered with straw. Birds in this case were toughened on free range before being brought on to verandas for the production of hatching eggs. This method produces very high egg yields, although Beltsvilles do well under most systems.

Turkey Yards

Turkeys do well in yards, managing quite well without any additional shelter. Most turkey fatteners do, however, give some protection from the weather as an aid to feed conversion efficiency and disease control. The birds in the picture, part of a smallholder's Christmas flock, are kept on pebbles—an excellent alternative to straw.

METHODS OF FEEDING

Correct feeding, both before and during the breeding season (from March onwards) has a great influence on fertility and hatchability. Nearly all the well-known feedingstuff compounders make special meals and pellets for turkeys and these should be purchased in preference to standard poultry mashes. Give a mash feed in the morning and grain in the late afternoon. A recommended home-mixed breeding mash is bran, 3 parts; wheat meal, 2 parts; barley meal, 2 parts; Sussex ground oats, 1 part; high protein grass meal, 1 part; white fish meal, 1 part. Add cod liver oil at 2 per cent.

Turkeys in small yards must be given daily supplies of greenfood in racks (*above*). If folded on young, leafy leys (*below*) they will find a considerable part of their own food. Fresh water must always be available. A guard to prevent the turkeys perching on the container and fouling the water is advisable.

BREEDING AND REARING

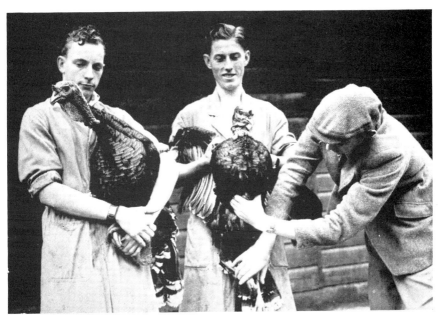

Stock Birds

Sᴛᴏᴄᴋ turkeys are best selected in October and November. Earlier than this it may be difficult to assess their true value. Chosen birds should have well-balanced bodies and long, straight breast bones. Heads should be of good depth; eyes bright and bold. Legs should be set wide apart. Photos show how turkeys can be held when examining for these points.

Year-old females may be used for breeding, providing they are well up to size. In this case, a young, vigorous stag should be run with them. The usual proportion is 1 stag to about 10 females for individual pens, and 1 to 15 when flock mating is practiced. These figures apply to the Bronze and English White and the ratio can be somewhat increased for the smaller breeds.

Assessing Value for Breeding

Besides handling to ascertain body size, stock turkeys should be weighed to make sure that they are up to standard for their breed. Bronze and English White females should weigh not less than 13 lb. For Norfolk Blacks, 10 lb.–12 lb. is a satisfactory figure: for Small Whites, 9–10 lb. Suspending each bird by the wings from a spring balance is the simplest method of weighing (*right*). Males should likewise be well up to weight, according to their age and breed, but exceptionally large birds are sometimes too heavy for young females and fertility may suffer.

Turkeys like to lay in a secluded spot and if trap nesting is adopted the nests should offer this (*below*). Regular trap nesting is really essential if egg yields and bodily conformation are to be improved and this policy has been largely responsible for the singular progress of English Whites. Flock mating and trap nesting should not be combined.

Weighing Stock Birds

Trap Nesting

Sun Parlour

Turkey breeding need not be confined to large farms where the stock can be given all the range they desire. It is true that disease is likely to occur under more intensive conditions if the birds are run on stale land, but there are ways of overcoming this problem. Small, wire-floored sun parlours are particularly useful as the turkeys never come in contact with the ground. They are simple to construct and are easily moved so that the droppings beneath can be cleared.

Enclosed runs are also satisfactory, providing they are used for no more than a year and are then ploughed, limed and reseeded. A pen of a dozen females and a stag (*below*) would need about ¼ acre under this system. Simple housing, giving 4 sq. ft. per bird, is sufficient. With both sun parlours and runs, the food and water vessel should be placed outside the enclosure so that the contents cannot be fouled. This also saves labour. If necessary guard against wild birds taking the food.

Enclosed Runs

Fitting Saddles

The fitting of saddles to turkey hens has two main advantages. They prevent damage to the hen by heavy stags (torn flesh is a very common occurrence otherwise) and if the saddles are numbered, ailing or broody birds can be identified quickly for subsequent action.

Strong canvas is used to make the saddles and the fronts are fitted on either side with loops which are passed over the birds' wings. They are still worth fitting even when damage has been done for they prevent the other birds pecking at the wound.

Breeding pens should be made up in January and the first eggs may be expected some time in March. First-year females lay a considerably greater number of eggs than second-year birds. These older birds should be marketed as soon as egg production ceases for there generally follows a rapid decline in weight.

It is quite in order for turkeys to hatch and rear their own chicks, though most breeders prefer to break broodiness in a slatted-floor coop so that laying may continue. If a turkey is used, give her a large coop, box or barrel (*below*) and up to 16 eggs. Take the usual precautions against rats and slightly moisten the eggs each day during the last ten days.

Hatching and Rearing

Both natural and artificial incubation give good results. Incubator management is much the same as for hens' eggs, except that extra moisture must be given during the last week of the 28 day period. Start the machine at 102°, gradually increasing to 103°.

Nine turkey eggs are sufficient for a broody hen. The coop should be fairly roomy and may be placed indoors or out, providing protection is given against rats. Indoor brooding (*below*) is favoured by some small breeders. Better still is a daily move on clean short grass.

Poults reared intensively need plenty of floor space. An initial allowance of 1 sq. ft. per bird should be increased by stages until they have 6 sq. ft. from 16 weeks onwards. Perches (*centre*) can be provided at the three-month stage. Sun parlours (*below*) are a great aid to health and should be provided whenever possible. If homemade, brace the floor well and cover with welded wire mesh.

Floor Space

Dry Food Saves Labour

To ensure correct balance, the use of a proprietary starter mash is advised. This is best given *ab lib* in hoppers as otherwise some eight feeds of wet mash must be given each day at first. Corn will be taken from an early age but should not be allowed to upset the balance of the diet. Change to a growers' mash at eight weeks.

Perches

Sun Parlour

"Carry-on" Brooder

A brooder temperature of 95° is required during the first week. After this the heat can be reduced gradually until weaning at six to eight weeks. The carry-on brooder above is suitable for the latter stages. Infra-red lamps for turkey rearing are becoming increasingly popular.

The Motley-type Veranda

A labour-saving means of housing growing turkeys which, by keeping them off the ground, goes far to prevent the ravages of blackhead, a parasitic disease causing heavy losses in young turkeys. Prevention and cure can also be effected by drugs obtainable in proprietary form.

Fattening Ration

It is worth feeding a special fattening ration during the last month before marketing. A watch must also be kept for fighting at this time, though this is less likely when the poults are given a little extra space to move around (*above*). Two mash feeds and one grain feed are given daily, using ground oats and milk if possible, or a mixture of ground oats,

Killing a Turkey

wheat meal and barley meal, together with 10 per cent meat meal. Fish meal may taint the carcase.

Turkeys may be marketed either alive or dead and plucked. Ascertain market needs well in advance of the date of disposal. Turkeys should be starved 24 hours before slaughter and may be killed by either of the methods recommended for chickens (*see p.* 113), the stick method being best for large birds. Hang the dead birds for five minutes and then pluck immediately.

GUINEA FOWL AND
BANTAMS

THE drive towards increased efficiency in egg- and table-bird production has tended to by-pass some of the less common branches of poultry-keeping. Yet these often offer very good returns for the enterprising smallholder who seeks his own markets and devises his own methods of efficient production. A case in point is the guinea fowl, long overlooked as a profit-maker but now being kept—sometimes in batteries—by quite a number of poultry-keepers. They often find it best to deal direct with hotels and restaurants.

Bantams, the miniatures of the poultry world, have a special appeal of their own. As exhibition birds, as pets or as household egg suppliers, they have no competitors where space is limited. Yet such is their attraction that they are quite a common sight in the yards of spacious farms.

GUINEA FOWL

GUINEA fowl are seldom kept in large numbers in this country but many farmers and smallholders run a few birds for their own table or to supply a small local demand. Adult guinea fowl pick up most of their own food and, like geese, they should not be kept under intensive conditions. They are fine watch dogs, sounding an alarm on the least provocation, and need no special housing. Trees and barns are the roosting places they prefer.

★

In contrast to their adult hardiness, the chicks require careful handling at first and must not be allowed to get wet. They are best reared by a hen in a coop and partly-covered run, but can have their freedom after four weeks. Feed as for ordinary chicks, though with a little more protein, starting with six feeds daily if wet mash is given.

★

Adult guinea fowl require a grain feed each evening all the year round and in addition, a morning feed of mash—during the winter at least. Much depends on the amount and type of range available. Food can be increased a little for the last month before killing.

★

The eggs of the guinea fowl are good to eat if not required for hatching but the hens must be watched carefully as they are experts at hiding their nests. Though having a reputation for wildness, many guinea fowl owners testify to their intelligence and friendliness. In short, they are an interesting addition to the holding and require little trouble or outlay.

BANTAMS

White Leghorns

BANTAMS are simply miniature editions of the normal types of fowl though some of the breeds and strains developed primarily for showing do differ somewhat in conformation from their large relatives. Pullets of many strains now lay 150 or more eggs in a year and there are laying trials especially for bantams. Typical bantam breeds are shown on this page.

Silver Pencilled Wyandotte

Minorca

Whether you wish to keep them for exhibition or to provide eggs for the household, bantams are fascinating little birds and require much less room and food than large fowls. The eggs are also smaller, of course, but at about 1¼ oz. each are well worth having. The fancy is a particularly keen one and there are many well-supported shows.

Neat Unit

Any neat, well-designed unit that is suitable for large fowls will suit bantams equally well, but about twice as many birds can be kept in the same space. Bantams are active little creatures and need a covered scratching space.

Feeding is just the same as for full-size birds except that very much less is needed. Because so little is required, household scraps go a long way towards providing for them.

When buying bantams, be quite clear as to your purpose—i.e., fancy or utility. Show birds are often poor egg-producers. On the other hand, do not start with nondescript stock, for many utility breeders are eventually lured by the skill, interest and friendly rivalry of show breeding.

INDEX

*Each section of the book (Poultry, Ducks, Geese and Turkeys),
is indexed under these headings.*

POULTRY

DUCKS

GEESE

TURKEYS